HOW TO CLIMB MT. BLANC IN A SKIRT

MICK CONEFREY

HOW TO CLIMB MT. BLANC IN A SKIRT

MICK CONEFREY

*A HANDBOOK FOR THE
LADY ADVENTURER*

palgrave
macmillan

Illustrations © Mick Conefrey
Illustrations by Adam T. Burton

First published in 2011 by PALGRAVE MACMILLAN® in the
U.S.—a division of St. Martin's Press LLC, 175 Fifth Avenue, New
York, NY 10010.

Where this book is distributed in the UK, Europe and the rest of the
world, this is by Palgrave Macmillan, a division of Macmillan
Publishers Limited, registered in England, company number 785998,
of Houndmills, Basingstoke, Hampshire RG21 6XS.

Palgrave Macmillan is the global academic imprint of the above
companies and has companies and representatives throughout the
world.

Palgrave® and Macmillan® are registered trademarks in the United
States, the United Kingdom, Europe and other countries.

ISBN: 978-0-230-10642-0

Library of Congress Cataloging-in-Publication Data
Conefrey, Mick.
    How to climb Mt. Blanc in a skirt : a handbook for the lady
adventurer / Mick Conefrey.
        p.   cm.
    ISBN 978-0-230-10642-0
    1. Women adventurers—Biography.   2. Women explorers—
Biography.   3. Women travelers—Biography.   4. Voyages and
travels—Anecdotes.   5. Women—Biography.   I. Title.
CT9970.C66   2011
910.82—dc22

                                                      2010035163

A catalogue record of the book is available from the British Library.

Design by Letra Libre

First edition: March 2011

10 9 8 7 6 5 4 3 2 1

Printed in the United States of America.

*To
Stella*

CONTENTS

PREFACE

A few years ago, after making a series of documentaries about mountaineering and Arctic exploration, I wrote *The Adventurer's Handbook,* in which I attempted to look at the history of exploration in a slightly unusual way. I wanted to discover the life lessons that could be drawn from the experiences of the great explorers and the archetypal patterns that most expeditions follow.

Most of the characters in that book were men. I have to come clean and admit that I was simply ignorant of the long history of female travelers and explorers. Some of them—for example, Amelia Earhart and Freya Stark—are still well known today, but none of them share the status of Ernest Shackleton, Roald Amundsen, or Reinhold Messner.

This book is a small attempt to redress the balance. Within these five chapters you'll find the stories of dozens of female explorers, sailors, pilots, and horsewomen. A few made careers out of exploration; others only made one great journey. Most were brave, some were reckless, and all were fascinating. So why are they not better known? Often they were just as heroic and just as eccentric as the men. There is no question that Osa Johnson, Jackie Cochran, and Wanda Rutkiewicz lived hugely exciting lives, but when it comes to exploration, women have rarely been accorded the same respect as men.

Until very recently, exploration was seen as an almost exclusively male realm; anyone who had the temerity to challenge that view was heading for trouble. Women found it harder to raise money, to get permissions to travel to remote areas, and to be taken seriously. In spite of this, hundreds of women did take to the air, the sea, and the dusty road to follow their dreams or simply go in search of adventure. But did they approach exploration differently from men? Were their concerns and obsessions the same? And do their stories have anything to say about the wider difference between the sexes?

This is a dangerous territory to get into. There is nothing harder than making generalizations about men and women, and no easier way to make a fool of yourself than by claiming to understand the difference between the genders. No sooner do you find a pattern than someone invariably comes along to contradict it.

Exploration, though, is all about risk, and to avoid this rather fascinating question would be to take the easy way out. So with a nod to Mary Hall, the Victorian world traveler, I have decided to follow her motto—"Take every precaution and abandon all fear"—and plunge deep into the dark continent of gender relations. My aim is to try to discover if there is a distinctly female approach to travel, and if so, what lessons can be learned from it.

First, though, a few words of gratitude to the people who have helped and supported me with this book. I would like to thank Christina Dodwell, Dominique Jean, Hugh Thompson, Amanda Faber, Carmel Conefrey, David Presswell, the staff of the Bodleian Library, the staff and trustees of the London Library, Anthony Sheil, Sally Riley and Leah Middleton at Aitken Alexander Ltd., Bettina Feldweg at Piper, Alessandra Bastagli at Palgrave Macmillan, and Mike Harpley at OneWorld. I would like to give special thanks to Adam T. Burton, who so beautifully illustrated this book. As ever, I owe a huge debt to my children, Frank and Phyllis, who put up with my absences, and most of all to my darling wife, Stella, without whose kindness and consideration this book could never have been written.

HOW TO CLIMB MT. BLANC IN A SKIRT

MICK CONEFREY

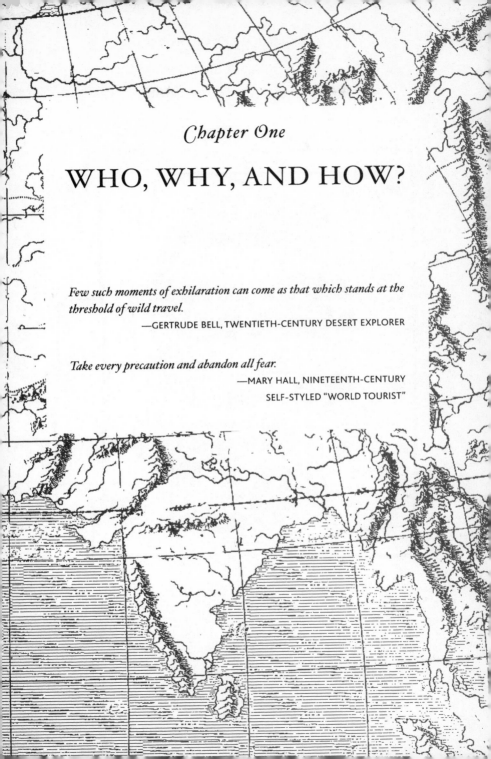

Chapter One

WHO, WHY, AND HOW?

Few such moments of exhilaration can come as that which stands at the threshold of wild travel.

—GERTRUDE BELL, TWENTIETH-CENTURY DESERT EXPLORER

Take every precaution and abandon all fear.

—MARY HALL, NINETEENTH-CENTURY
SELF-STYLED "WORLD TOURIST"

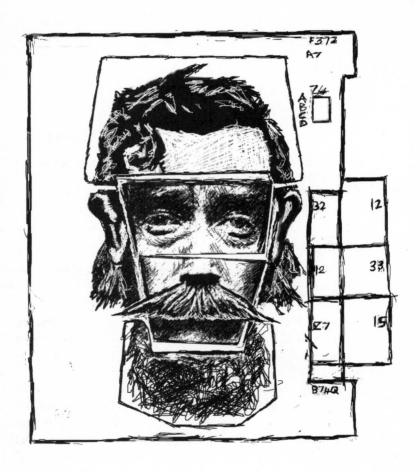

WHO?

Ask someone to describe a typical explorer and they will usually have a pretty good idea. Explorers have lined faces, scraggy beards, skin that has been punished by the wind and sun. Sometimes they wear furs; sometimes they wear khaki. They either smile at the camera in triumph or they stare with gritty resolution.

And they are men.

Or are they?

Which explorer found the lost city of Cana in the Middle East?

Which mountaineer first mapped the Siachen Glacier in the Himalayas?

Who was first to the top of Huascarán in Peru?

Which European was first to visit the Ottoman harem in Constantinople?

Who held the world record for the fastest flight from Britain to Australia for 44 years?

You'll find the answers to all of these questions within these pages, and none of the protagonists will have a scraggy beard. This book is about female explorers and travelers. Who were they? What did they achieve? And what can we learn from them?

The lost history of female exploration includes women who traveled to every corner of the globe: mountaineers like Fanny Bullock Workman and Annie Smith Peck, sailors like Ann Davison and Naomi James, desert explorers such as Rosita Forbes and Freya Stark, polar explorers such as Ann Bancroft and Pam Flowers, and "African queens" such as May French Sheldon and Mary Kingsley. A handful of them are still well known today, some enjoyed just a few fleeting months in the headlines, and others never saw the limelight at all.

Of course, for most of them, fame was not what spurred them into a life of exploration. They were not traveling for posterity; they were driven by what Martin Luther King called the "fierce urgency of now."

Ella Maillart didn't make incredible journeys through central Asia hoping to join Ernest Shackleton and Robert Falcon Scott in the pantheon of great explorers; she did it because she was desperately excited to encounter other cultures. It would be a tragedy, though, if the exploits of Maillart and the other great women explorers were forgotten. Their stories are just as entertaining and just as inspiring as any of the more familiar exploration tales.

We'll begin, though, by posing the question that no explorer likes to hear:

WHY?

For most adventurers and travelers, male or female, the answer to "why?" is a complex mixture of desires and emotions, often combined with a lot of vagueness and happenstance. "Because it is there," in order to go beyond "the far blue mountains" or "the far horizon" are just some of the many stock answers trotted out by reluctant interviewees who cannot or do not want to explain their wanderlust. This is an important question, though, for anyone trying to look at the differences between male and female travelers, so it is worth a closer look.

Some reasons are common to both sexes. Isabella Bird, for example, was one of several people who first went abroad for health reasons. At home in Victorian Britain, she was a virtual invalid who suffered from insomnia, spinal prostration, boils, severe headaches, hair loss, muscular spasms, and depression. But once on the trail, she was transformed into a fearless adventurer and expert horsewoman who traveled all around the world, from Australia, to Japan, to Hawaii, to the Rocky Mountains and the deserts of Kurdistan.

The British journalist Beatrix Bulstrode was one of many explorers who went in search of an alternative to modern civilization. She made an expedition to the wilds of Mongolia in 1913, hoping to "revert to the primitive," only to discover that, after a couple of months, the primitive had become "rather predictable."

The American aviatrix Amelia Earhart was one of the few people who confessed her motivation, though undoubtedly it was shared by

many others. As her autobiography proclaimed, she made a series of daring, long-distance plane journeys quite simply for the fun of it.

You'll find versions of the common "whys" in the biographies of both male and female explorers, but there are some answers that seem to be more gender specific.

WHY WOMEN EXPLORE

For Womankind?

No man ever climbed a mountain or crossed a river to prove what a man could do, though several might have done it for *Mankind*, with a capital *M*. For women, it has been different. To a much greater extent, they were going against expectations and trespassing in a male realm. Some

politely ignored this, but others saw their successes and failures very much in terms of gender. Alexandra David-Néel wrote that she made her famous journey to Lhasa in 1924 to show what "the will of a woman could do." A decade earlier, the American mountaineer Fanny Bullock Workman was photographed on top of a mountain pass in the Karakoram, holding up a banner calling for "Votes for Women." It would be a mistake, however, to think that all female explorers were feminists. In fact, some were at pains to point out the opposite. Gertrude Bell, one of the most famous women travelers of the early twentieth century, was a founder member of the British Women's Anti-Suffrage League. And more recent women, from the mountaineer Julie Tullis to the sailor Clare Francis, have written about their dislike of so-called women's lib.

To Change Sex

Apart from Jan, née James, Morris, the famous travel writer who had a sex change operation in the early 1970s, few male explorers have had to deal with complex gender identity issues. To put it more simply, not very many of them have had to spend a lot of time dressed up as women. However, several notable women throughout history had to pass themselves off as men, and not just for a day. Stella Court Treatt drove all the way through Africa from the Cape to Cairo in the 1920s dressed as a boy. Isabelle Eberhardt wandered around North Africa disguised as an Arab scholar, and Lady Hester Stanhope spent much of her strange life decked out like a well-to-do Turkish merchant. For most of these women, cross-dressing was a necessary evil that facilitated their travel, but in the behavior of certain women, you sometimes get a whiff of something more transgressive. Dressing as men made their travels smoother, but it also gave them the opportunity to explore their sexuality and gender. When Sarah Hobson trekked around Iran masquerading as a young British man, not only was she propositioned by Iranian women and their fathers who saw her as a good catch for their daughters, but she also found herself flirting with local girls and enjoying the crude jokes of the men she hung out with. Isabelle Eberhardt certainly had a very complex and active sex life, and she clearly enjoyed playing with gender and identity.

For the Sake of Their Dead Husbands

There are no male explorers who traveled for the sake of their wives' reputation, but a small and fascinating group of women took to the trail to settle their dead husbands' unfinished business. In 1903, for example, Mina Hubbard became the first person to cross Labrador in Canada by canoe. It took considerable guts: her husband, Leonidas, had starved to death on his attempt. Not only did Mina Hubbard have to battle against the environment, but she also had to race against her husband's old friends who were determined to beat her to the prize. Similarly, Ruth Harkness, a New York socialite and fashion designer, went to China in 1936, aiming to bring the first live panda back to the United States. Her husband, Bill, had died in Shanghai earlier that year, having spent 13 frustrating months trying to capture the mythical creature. Like Mina Hubbard, Ruth Harkness had to contend with one of her husband's former partners who had set up a rival expedition. After several weeks of difficult going, she and her team managed to capture a baby panda; Harkness then had the equally tough job of nursing furry little Su-Lin all the way back to Chicago.

To Lose Weight!

Several women travelers and mountaineers commented wryly in their memoirs that exploration and adventure are good for weight loss. For example, Caroline Hamilton and the four British women who trekked to the South Pole in 2000 lost a total of 97 pounds, the equivalent weight of the smallest member of their team. However, as Caroline and the others all noted, any fat lost on the ice invariably makes a comeback as soon as you return home.

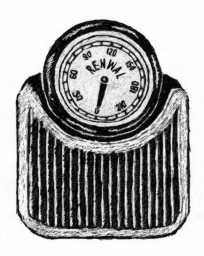

If there is an underlying theme in women's "whys," it is the idea of escape. Home often meant rigid social conventions, and traveling abroad offered the possibility of reinventing yourself.

WHY MEN EXPLORE

For King and Country

When Caroline Hamilton and an intrepid team of British women reached the South Pole in January 2000, they sang the national anthem, much to the amusement of scientists at a nearby American base.

They were the exception that proved the rule. Patriotism has rarely been a motivation for women explorers, although it has frequently been a very important one for men. In the nineteenth century, exploration was often seen as part of the empire-building strategies of the colonial powers, and no explorer's pack was complete without his national flag, to be raised at the top of the mountain, the end of the river, or the apex of the pole. Looking through their expedition accounts, it is clear that occasionally women travelers did (and still do) play the patriotic card—principally in order to raise money—but, comparing male and female travelers as a whole, nationalistic rivalry seems like much more of a male trait.

To Suffer

A lot of exploration books written by men include passages of what can be best described as "painography": long, detailed descriptions of suffering endured by the author. With some, you almost suspect that pain is part of the pleasure. Wilfred Thesiger, the desert explorer, for example, loved to describe the minimal rations and physical privations of his travels, and Roald Amundsen claimed that he was inspired set off for the Arctic after reading about the suffering of previous polar explorers. Few women, if any, match Thesiger's or Amundsen's relish for suffering. Many did experience pain and discomfort, but in their accounts they rarely dwell on it. Ida Pfeiffer, the nineteenth-century Viennese globe-trotter, walked through the jungles of Sumatra in bare feet because she could not find suitable shoes! At night, her guides used to lever thorns out of her soles with their machetes, but she never mentioned whether it hurt or not. There is no equivalent in women's exploration to the archetypal scene when the American polar explorer Robert Peary cuts off his frostbitten toes with a penknife and carves Hannibal's motto, "I shall find a way or make one," on the wall of his miserable wooden hut. Masochism seems to be a very male predilection.

First-ism

"First-ism" was, and still is, one of the most common motivations for alpha male explorers. They race to the poles, to the source of the Nile,

to the top of Everest and the bottom of the Arctic Ocean, aiming to get into the history books ahead of their rivals. Certainly there were, and still are, women who want to be remembered as the first to achieve something but, as with patriotism, this does not seem to have been quite such an important issue. Perhaps the truth is that women weren't really prone to first-ism because by the time they entered the race, the first prizes had already been taken. Or perhaps, like the great Swiss explorer Ella Maillart, they love travel for its own sake, not because they feel the need to assert themselves over others. Being the first *woman* to climb Everest or cross the Sahara has never had quite the same cachet as being the first *person* to do it. First-ism sometimes was a factor when women were trying to raise money, but in general, women explorers don't seem to have the same obsessive competitiveness as men.

Ultimately, whatever the "why" there are certain basic "hows" that have to be attended to before an expedition begins. Money has to be raised, teams have to be assembled, and equipment has to be procured; all of this is common for any adventurer, but, again, there are frequently differences in approach between genders.

FAMOUS SECONDS

SECOND WOMAN TO CLIMB MONT BLANC
In 1838 the French aristocrat Henriette D'Angeville claimed to have been the "first lady" to climb Mont Blanc. Not true. In her account, she didn't even mention her predecessor, the peasant girl Maria Paradis (who made the first female ascent in 1809).

SECOND WOMAN TO CLIMB EVEREST
Mrs. Phantog, a native Tibetan, was a member of the Chinese team that scaled Everest from the Tibetan side in the summer of 1975, 11 days after the Japanese climber Junko Tabei became the first woman to reach the summit. Initially, many Western climbers were very suspicious of their ascent. Proof came a few months later when a British team found a Chinese surveying marker that had been left at the top of Everest.

SECOND WOMAN INTO SPACE
The Soviet cosmonaut Svetlana Yevgenyevna was the second woman in space, and the first to make a space walk, 19 years after Valentina Tereshova and 7 months before Sally Ride, the first American female astronaut.

SECOND WOMEN TO REACH THE SOUTH POLE
The first women to reach the South Pole were scientists who flew there in 1969, but the first to get there under their own steam were Victoria Murden and Shirley Metz, who were among a party that skied to the pole 20 years later in 1989.

SECOND WOMAN TO SAIL AROUND THE WORLD SINGLE-HANDED
Between September 1977 and June 1978, the novice New Zealand yachtswoman Naomi James made an amazing single-handed voyage around the world, seemingly unaware of her Polish rival, Krystyna Chojnowska-Liskiewicz, who had in fact started more than a year earlier.

HOW TO RAISE MONEY

Raising money is one of those tedious but necessary endeavors that invariably require more time and effort than anyone anticipates. History has shown that it is much easier for men, and that women have found it hard to get government (and particularly military) funding. Today things are a little easier, but corporate sponsors often are reluctant to fund women's expeditions, either because they think that female teams are less likely to succeed or from sheer prejudice.

Nevertheless, one way or another, women have found a way to pay their way.

By Getting a Laugh

In 1978, the American mountaineer Arlene Blum put together an expedition to Annapurna in the Himalayas. Faced with a projected bill for $80,000, she and her team initially turned to the usual fundraising strategies: holding dinners, balls, and concerts and selling bumper stickers. None of these yielded much cash, but then someone came up with the bright idea of selling an expedition T-shirt, and someone

---

£64 7s. 10d
To travel from Dunkirk to Delhi by bicycle (personal savings)
—DERVLA MURPHY, 1963

£ 3,350
To buy a yacht fit for a solo crossing of the Atlantic (the bank of Mom and Dad)
—NICOLETTE MILNES WALKER, 1971

$500,000
To rent a plane to fly from Cape Town to the Antarctic (corporate sponsorship)
—THE ARNESEN-BANCROFT TRANS ANTARCTIC EXPEDITION, 2001

else came up with the even brighter idea of using the slogan: "A Woman's Place Is on Top . . . of Annapurna." Its mixture of humor and sexual assertion was perfect for the times; Blum and her team managed to sell over 15,000 T-shirts, which went a long way toward financing their expedition.

By Not Looking the Part

In 1937, the Anglo-Italian explorer Freya Stark was trying to fund a joint archaeological and cultural expedition to Arabia. She was advised to visit Baron "Cheers" Wakefield of Hythe, the millionaire behind Castrol Oil, who had a reputation for sponsoring women's expeditions. When she paid him a call, Lord Wakefield wasn't in the least interested in talking about archaeology or Arab culture, but he was very eager to show Stark photographs of all the famous people he had met. She listened patiently, flirted gently, and charmed him into handing over £1,500, in those days a significant sum. Afterward, Lord Wakefield told a friend that he'd offered her the money not because he liked the idea of the expedition but because Freya Stark looked so *unlike* his idea of an explorer.

By Crying a Lot

After failing on her first attempt to traverse Antarctica in 1993, Ann Bancroft returned to the United States $450,000 in debt, which took her many years to pay off. So when in 1998 she decided to make another attempt, she took on professional fundraisers Charlie Hartwell and Sarah and Fred Haberman. However, even with full time organisers on board, Anne still struggled to raise money. Faced with frequent and intensely frustrating rejection, she and her team found themselves bursting into tears during meetings. Eventually, however, what they dubbed "the crying tour" paid off, and they raised the $1.5 million necessary to make the expedition a reality. It took a lot of effort and a lot of tissues.

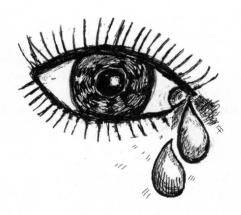

HOW TO DEAL WITH THE PRESS

I don't care what anyone writes about me, so long as it isn't true.

—DOROTHY PARKER

Publicity often goes hand in hand with sponsorship, but beware: The press has always been a fickle friend to explorers. The only thing journalists like more than creating heroes and heroines is destroying them . . . or at least poking a little fun. This is particularly the case when it comes to women, who frequently have been seen as either victims or viragos.

When, in 1908, the British novelist Charlotte Mansfield announced that she was about to set off on a perilous expedition to Africa, one editor asked if she might agree to get lost for six weeks and then give him an exclusive on her "rescue." Another sent a telegram asking if she wouldn't mind asking several leading suffragettes to accompany her.

TIPS FOR DEALING WITH THE PRESS

DON'T MIX PHOTOGRAPHERS AND BOYFRIENDS
British yachtswoman Clare Francis got a lot of press after her solo crossing of the Atlantic in 1973. Most journalists were very respectful, but one photographer insisted that she should pose in a bikini for some "action shots" on her yacht. He did not realize that Clare's boyfriend, Jacques Redon, was also on board; when he heard the photographer's demands, Redon quickly came up on deck and sent the man running for the quayside.

DON'T LET PRESS ADULATION GO TO YOUR HEAD
When New Zealander Jean Batten made her epic flight from England to New Zealand in 1936, she was lionized by the press. She, for her part, tried

to milk her fame for all it was worth and took to charging her fans for autographs. She even boasted to one friend that her name was so valuable that if she wrote a check, no one would ever cash it. When, however, she sold her story to a local newspaper syndicate, it was so ferocious about protecting its exclusive rights that it wouldn't let the public anywhere near her. Batten suffered such severe withdrawal symptoms from public adulation that she broke off her publicity tour and headed straight for a sanatorium for a well-earned nervous breakdown.

DON'T TRAVEL BY NIGHT

When, in 1958, three British women—Antonia Deacock, Anne Davies, and Eve Sims—put together an expedition to the remote region of Zanskar, in the Indian Himalayas, they got a lot of rather patronizing press coverage as "housewife mountaineers." They didn't mind too much because it brought in much-needed sponsorship, but at one press conference in Pakistan, arranged by Brooke Bond Tea, they found themselves in unexpected hot water. "Why," local journalists asked, "did you travel through Pakistan mainly at night? Is our country not beautiful enough to look at?" Of course, the reality was that the women had avoided driving during the day because it was so hot, but this was a reminder that the press often goes out of its way to make mischief.

Gwen Richardson had to struggle hard to avoid sensational coverage of her expedition to British Guiana in 1924. On her return, one New York journalist was so desperate to find a "victim" angle for her that he asked her to first claim that she had been kidnapped and anointed queen by local Indians. When Richardson demurred, he asked that she declare that "savages" had tried to kill her. She refused to play along but did provide him with a photograph in which she posed with her automatic pistol. It appeared in the paper next day, under the headline "The Deadly Bushmaster Snake that She Caught Alive." The gun had been air-brushed out and replaced with the image of a large snake, coiled around Richardson's arm.

At the other end of the spectrum, women with children often have found themselves almost vilified in the press when they embark on risky expeditions. During her life and after her death, the British climber Alison Hargreaves was frequently accused of selfishness for going on high-altitude expeditions and leaving her young children behind. Male explorers, by contrast, are never criticized for leaving their families to go off on expeditions, however perilous.

HOW TO TRAIN

How much time should you devote to pre-expedition training? This has always been a somewhat awkward question for explorers, male and female. Some take training very seriously while others virtually ignore it. Today it is possible to prepare scientifically if you can afford a gym and a personal coach, but less orthodox methods can also be effective.

STAND-UPS

The American polar explorer Pam Flowers prepared for her trans-Arctic dog-sled expedition in 1993 by hiking, chopping wood, lifting weights, and . . . getting rid of all the chairs in her cabin. She knew that she was going to have stand or walk for most of the next few months, so she decided to get used to long hours standing up.

"TIRING" YOURSELF OUT

Liv Arnesen, the Norwegian polar explorer, prepared for her epic solo trip across Antarctica by running around her hometown hauling a brace of tires behind her. Her neighbors were intrigued. When she told them that she was about to sled across the frozen wastes of the Antarctic, she found to her surprise that, rather than being shocked by the idea, a lot of them wanted to share their own travel fantasies.

HIGH KICKS AND DRIVEN PUNCHES

Julie Tullis, the British mountaineer, kept fit between expeditions by practicing martial arts. At first, the fearless mountaineer had been reluctant to join a class, because she was embarrassed by her bunions, but the more involved she became the more connections she saw between climbing and martial arts. In both cases, maximum success came when mind and body were moving in perfect flow. On a more practical level, in 1984 she once used her martial arts skill to literally punch her way out of an avalanche on Broad Peak in Pakistan.

HOW TO CHOOSE
CLOTHES AND EQUIPMENT

When it comes to equipment and clothing, it is noticeable that male and female explorer's generally seem to conform to stereotypical roles—men are often obsessed with gadgets, spending a lot of time preparing and commissioning equipment; women meanwhile, mention equipment and technology infrequently but do spend a lot of time thinking about what they are going to wear.

Some women commissioned specially designed clothes for their expeditions. When British traveler Beryl Smeeton made a long journey through China in the mid-1930s, she was determined to travel third class as much as possible in order to see the "real Orient." This meant no privacy, so she had a special overdress, made from kimono cloth, that she described as a tent with a hole at the top. There was enough

JOSEPHINE PEARY'S CLOTHING LIST
FOR AN EXPEDITION TO GREENLAND IN 1891

INSIDE CLOTHES
Knitted kidney protector
Jaros combination suit
Two knitted skirts
Flannel wrapper
Pair of knitted stockings
Pair of deer-skin moccasins

OUTSIDE CLOTHES
Great Fur overall
Muff
Snow shoes

GERTRUDE BELL'S CLOTHING LIST FOR
HER EXPEDITION TO HAYYIL IN ARABIA IN 1913

12 linen skirts
12 white shirts
A set of riding skirts
Riding boots
Evening dresses
Evening shoes
Silk underwear
Parasols
12 linen and straw hats
Fur coat
Woolen cardigans
Tweed traveling suits

room inside to change her underwear discreetly, and it was comfortable enough to wear for socializing and the all-important drinking of tea. When she wore it on a boat journey up the Yangtze River, the other passengers were so impressed that one man dragged his wife over and put Smeeton's tent dress on himself to demonstrate its virtues.

Isabella Bird, one of Victorian Britain's most intrepid travelers, commissioned a special bloomer suit for her famous expedition through the Rocky Mountains. When in town she usually rode side-saddle, but on the trail she sat astride the horse and sported her bloomer suit—basically a pair of baggy trousers with a split skirt sewn on top. When an article in the *Times* of London implied that she wore men's clothing, Bird threatened to sue.

Once you're suited, booted, cash-flowed, publicized, trained, motivated, and challenged, it is time for the real work to begin. The next chapter introduces the leading women explorers and the places they visited.

But first, a vital issue for any traveler . . .

HOW TO SURVIVE
WITHOUT TOILET PAPER

It's different for girls. Men can discreetly unzip and let fly. For women, going to the bathroom is a more complicated business—so complicated, in fact, that some women have made themselves ill by holding it in.

Victorians did not mention their toilet habits, but modern women have no such compunction. In Julie Tullis's climbing memoir, she graphically recounts an episode of projectile diarrhea on K2. In Caroline Hamilton's expedition book, she recalls how on her trip to the South Pole, all her companions became fascinated by their bodily excretions.

In between the silence of the Victorian era and the surplus detail of today's adventurers, there are more veiled references. Beryl Smeeton found that her "tent dress" was also useful for hiding "a woman's most basic functions," and Alexandra David-Néel admitted to urinating in her peasant dress on the road to Lhasa.

For the pioneering female aviators of the nineteen-thirties, wearing a skirt was no help. Male pilots used pee bottles, but women found them awkward and uncomfortable. When cheeky journalists asked the famously beautiful New Zealander Jean Batten, the "Garbo of the Air," about the toilet issue, she would fend them off by claiming that she had trained herself to drink very little water prior to flights. In fact, she had a top-secret modification to her De Havilland Moth. Concealed by a cushion, there was a toilet pipe in the middle of her seat; it could be opened and closed by means of a trapdoor below the fuselage operated from within the cabin.

So much for aerial evacuations, but what does one do when the toilet paper runs out? There have been many ingenious solutions:

Snowballs?

When the Irish writer Dervla Murphy and her six-year-old daughter, Rachel, went to Baltistan in the 1970s, their toilet paper quickly ran out. They found that snow was a useful, though cold, alternative, but things got a little difficult at lower altitudes when it became slush mixed with rock.

The Classics?

When the Swiss explorer Ella Maillart journeyed through the Soviet Union in 1932, creature comforts were in short supply. A traveler's edition of Balzac proved to be excellent toilet reading, both for its narra-tive and its absorbent qualities.

Sticky Stuff?

Spare a thought for Marie Herbert, wife of Wally Herbert, the polar explorer. On her first day in the Arctic, she retreated into a shed to deal with a call of nature and conveniently discovered a roll of what she thought was toilet paper, only to discover that she had picked up a roll of self-adhesive insulating tape. Ouch.

Chapter Two

WHERE?

*Rhodesia wants women, needs women; in fact women and women only
can insure its future prosperity. . . . My advice is, treble the tax on whisky
and import women free of charge.*

—CHARLOTTE MANSFIELD, TWENTIETH-CENTURY
NOVELIST AND TRAVELER

There is a certain madness that comes over one at the mere sight of a map.

—FREYA STARK, TWENTIETH-CENTURY TRAVELER

*There's a big difference between seeing a crocodile from the deck of a
steamer lying picturesquely on a mud bank and from the vantage point
of a small dug out canoe—he is highly interesting and you may not be
able to write home about him.*

—MARY KINGSLEY, NINETEENTH-CENTURY TRAVELER

The simple answer to the question "where?" is "everywhere." Today there are very few parts of the world that haven't been explored by women. From the tops of the highest mountains, to depths of the world's deepest caves, women have been there.

The heyday of female exploration ran from the middle of the nineteenth century to the middle of the twentieth. During those one hundred years, women such as Mary Kingsley, Alexandra David-Néel, and Gertrude Bell became world famous for their expeditions to Africa, Asia, and the Middle East. There were, however, some regions — most notably the Arctic and the Antarctic — that have been penetrated by women only relatively recently. The main reason for this is financial. It takes an awful lot of money to mount an expedition to the North or South Pole, and in the past women simply didn't have sufficient resources. As Freya Stark proved, though, it was possible to conduct small-scale but important expeditions to the Middle East on very limited budgets.

THE DESERT

Some of the most celebrated women explorers made their names in the deserts of North Africa and the Middle East: Freya Stark, Gertrude Bell, Rosita Forbes, Hester Stanhope, Isabelle Eberhardt, Ella Sykes, Isabella Bird . . . the list goes on.

Deserts, however, were extremely dangerous places to explore. Besides the environmental hazards, there was the ever-present risk of sudden violence. In most of North Africa and the Middle East, foreigners were outsiders, called *ferenghi, nasrani,* or "infidels," who should be put to the sword or, at least, robbed. Raiding parties might appear on the horizon at any moment. If the travelers were lucky, one of their guides might recognize a friend or relative, and then everyone would end up sharing a pot of coffee. If they were unlucky, they might lose all their goods, or worse. The Swiss traveler Isabelle Eberhardt was attacked by a saber-wielding religious fanatic who almost cut off her arm. Alexine Tinné was less fortunate; she was killed by Tuareg raiders in the Sahara.

The dangers undoubtedly kept many explorers away from the Middle East, but, for others, they only added to the excitement. Anglo-Italian traveler Freya Stark called risk the "salt and sugar of life," but the desert offered much more than the occasional frisson of fear. It had everything: history, culture, extraordinary landscapes, and both physical and spiritual challenges.

PERSIAN TRAVEL TIPS

When leaving for a long journey . . .
> . . . always begin on your left foot.
> . . . exit your house facing the door.
> . . . give money to beggars, especially female beggars.
> . . . it is bad luck to sneeze once, but it is not so bad if you sneeze two or three times.
> . . . say "Mashallah" *(May Allah will it)* but do not look at a child or an animal.

—AS COMPILED BY ELLA SYKES, BRITISH TRAVELER

1716–1718: Lady Mary Montagu Visits Constantinople

Lady Mary Wortley Montagu was a larger-than-life British aristocrat, a society beauty, and a witty sparring partner of the poet Alexander Pope. In 1716 she accompanied her husband, the British ambassador, to the Ottoman court in Constantinople. On her return, she published what she claimed to be the first authentic account of life in a harem, scorning previous travel writers as "men who had written about what they didn't know." She was fascinated by Eastern sensuality, and her long description of Turkish women lounging naked in the bathhouse titillated and scandalized eighteenth-century Britain.

1810: Lady Hester Stanhope Is Shipwrecked en Route to Cairo

Lady Hester Stanhope was the niece of the British prime minister William Pitt. She was a famous hostess who spent her 20s presiding over the drawing rooms of 10 Downing Street before heading off to see the world with a retinue of servants, doctors, and lovers. Stanhope planned to settle in Cairo but was shipwrecked close to the island of Rhodes. She lost all her luggage and had to adopt local clothing, but she so enjoyed the freedom it gave her that she spent most of the remainder of her life dressed like a flamboyant Turkish merchant.

The high point of her travels came in 1813, when she set off across the Syrian Desert to Palmyra, the ancient city built by Solomon and ruled over by the legendary queen Zenobia. When she arrived, local people proclaimed her their queen, thus fulfilling the prophecy of the

British spiritualist Richard Brothers that one day she would reign over the East. After several weeks, however, Stanhope grew bored of Palmyra and returned to the coast, where she had the bad luck to catch the plague. She survived and spent the rest of her days living near to ancient city of Sidon, attempting to rule over local people and becoming known as a mystic. "Europe," she said, "is boring."

HOW TO SPOT A GOOD CAMEL

Get the camel to kneel. Put your foot on its thigh. If it can stand up without assistance, it is a good camel.

—LADY ANNE BLUNT

1878: Lady Anne Blunt Explores Arabia

In 1878, Lady Anne Blunt, granddaughter of the famous British poet Lord Byron, became the first European woman to travel through central Arabia. She traveled with her husband, the horse-breeder and poet Wilfred Blunt, and a small Arab retinue. Their fascinating journey took them from the wild beauty of Nejd desert to the remote city of Hayyil, which was reputed to have the best-preserved stud farm in Arabia.

The Blunts were fearless and hugely resilient. They traveled light, living off what they could buy and what they could hunt. Lady Anne's notes on desert cuisine were characteristically detailed and unsqueamish.

LOCUST

Catch them: In the morning when they are so cold that their wings freeze up.

Cook them: Locusts are best boiled, then dipped in salt.

Taste: More like vegetable than meat.

Tip: Red locusts are more tasty than green.

HYENA

Catch them: Hyenas can be hunted conventionally with dogs and guns and are surprisingly easy to corner.

Cook them: Hyenas taste best when roasted; country hyenas have a very thick fatty layer on the inside of their skin, so they do need a lot of time on the spit.

Taste: Lady Anne wasn't partial to hyena, but her husband and her Arab servants were keen.

1890: Isabella Bird Explores Persia and Kurdistan

In the early 1890s, Isabella Bird, then Europe's most famous woman explorer, made an exhausting winter expedition to Persia and Kurdistan. She was meticulous and well organized. On either side of her saddle she wore two large holsters: one with a loaded revolver, the other with tea-making equipment. She began her journey through Persia in the dead of winter and suffered terribly from the cold even though she wore two coats, a jacket, and a mountain dress. Bird's fame meant nothing to local people, who treated her with hostility. She was not allowed to touch anything in the bazaar, lest her Christian hand should pollute it. She in turn was very critical of what she saw, in particular the way in which females were treated: She wrote that rich women were led around on asses and tended to by eunuchs; poor women looked like hags by the age of 20.

Hidden Dangers of the Desert

The Cold

The highest temperature ever measured on land was 136 degrees Fahrenheit, 58 degrees Celsius; this record was set in 1922 at El Azizia in the Libyan Sahara. Deserts, however, can also get very cold. At night, temperatures can drop below freezing, and daily highs and lows can vary enormously. When Isabella Bird traveled through Persia, the mornings were so cold that her ink froze in its bottle and her washbowl frequently iced over before she had a chance to bathe. She wore three pairs of gloves and a six-layer face mask, but nothing could protect her from the vicious wind. Bird did have a recommendation though for future travelers: Take double peppermint lozenges to ward off the cold.

Sandfly Fever

Isabella Bird also warned her readers of the dangers of sandfly fever, commonly known as Baghdad boils. It is transmitted by female sand-flies, which carry tiny, single-cell parasites called Leishmania. Weeks, sometimes months, after being bitten, ugly burnlike welts appear on a victim's skin. They can take up to year to heal, frequently leaving large scars. In the worst cases, the parasites bury themselves in their victim's internal organs, where they wreak havoc. Leishmaniasis remains the second most dangerous parasitic disease in the world after malaria, killing up to half a million people every year.

Flash Floods

Though by definition there is very low precipitation in a desert, when the rains come, they can come very quickly. The early-twentieth-century British traveler Ella Sykes was one of many travelers who waxed lyrical about the desert being carpeted by flowers after a storm, but sudden downpours can also be very dangerous. In 1904, Isabelle Eberhardt, the Swiss traveler, was killed by a flash flood in Algeria, when her mud house collapsed after being hit by a torrent of water. She was found wedged under the staircase, with her arms over her head, vainly trying to protect herself. Flash floods most commonly occur in dry areas that are suddenly inundated with rain. The ground becomes saturated very quickly, and the rainfall has nowhere to go but downhill, followed by dirt and debris.

1913–1914: Gertrude Bell Journeys to Hayyil, Arabia

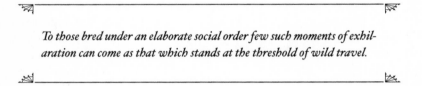

To those bred under an elaborate social order few such moments of exhilaration can come as that which stands at the threshold of wild travel.

The first truly great female desert explorer was Britain's Gertrude Bell. A skilled linguist, a respected archaeologist, cartographer, historian, ethnographer, alpinist, and government adviser, Bell was a hugely impressive woman. She was also, however, a singularly tortured individual: a passionate, intensely romantic figure who died a virgin when she overdosed on sleeping pills just before her fifty-eighth birthday.

Gertrude Bell came from a family of successful British industrialists and rarely wanted for money. She lavished much of her wealth on travel; by the age of 34, she had been around the world twice, visiting everywhere from Tokyo to Constantinople. The Middle East was her real passion, though. She made her first extended visit there in 1900 and eventually settled in Baghdad, the capital city of Iraq, a new country whose borders she had helped to delineate.

Bell made many epic journeys through the desert, but perhaps her most courageous expedition was in 1913, when she traveled from Baghdad to Hayyil in the middle of Arabia. Unlike her earlier archaeological field trips, this was a journey that had no ostensible motive, except one: to prove that she was up to the challenge.

During the preceding year, Bell had fallen madly in love with a dashing British officer, Dick Doughty-Wylie. But there was a problem: Dick was married. The two managed to spend several torrid days together in London and filled their correspondence with passionate yearning, but they never consummated their relationship, and Bell realized that there was little prospect of Dick divorcing his wife. So she left him and set off for the desert, aiming to replicate a journey made 50 years earlier by one of Doughty-Wylie's uncles, the famous geologist Charles Doughty.

Hayyil was the home of the Rashids, one of the two most powerful tribes in Arabia. For many years, the Rashids had been at war with the Sauds, Britain's principal ally in the region. Bell was essentially heading into enemy territory, and neither the British government nor the Turkish authorities, who were then nominally in control of Arabia, supported her expedition. Not only would she have to travel over 600 miles of difficult terrain, but she would have to negotiate the complex politics and unpredictable violence of the desert tribes alone, relying only on traditional Arabian hospitality to keep her safe.

Experience had taught her that the best way to deal with warlords and dignitaries was to impress upon them her status, so as you can see from the list on the next page, Bell traveled in grand style.

From the outset it was a difficult, tense journey. Bell paid handsomely for "rafiqs"—guides from the tribes whose land she was crossing. Their presence was supposed to protect her caravan from attack, but six days in she got her first taste of the dangers that lay ahead when her party was attacked by Druze raiders.

Bell was forced off her camel, her servants were beaten, and her saddlebags were emptied onto the sand. It looked as if they would be stripped of everything when suddenly her tent boy recognized one of the attackers and publicly denounced him for bad faith. Hadn't they

GERTRUDE BELL'S EQUIPMENT LIST

A tent for sleeping and bathing
A tent for eating and writing
Two cameras
Compasses
A folding bath
A folding bed
A folding chair
Silver candlesticks
Cigarette holders
Cigarette Cases

traded camels last year? Shouldn't they be treated like friends? Amazingly, the raiders stopped and handed everything back.

The episode was a brutal and slightly surreal taste of things to come. Some Arabs treated Bell with great hospitality while others menaced her into handing over gifts and money. It is hard to imagine what they really made of her: an independent woman traveling alone except for her servants; a woman who could speak fluent Arabic, recite tomes of Islamic poetry, and who seemed to know more about their country than they did. She was most definitely not what they were used to.

In spite of the danger, Bell always enjoyed her encounters with Arab life and was particularly interested to meet nomadic Bedouin tribes. For the first time in her career as a desert explorer, she was able to spend a lot of time with Arab women in harems and witness their strange, cloistered existence. It was not a particularly edifying experience.

As the journey progressed, the expedition grew to over 30 people, with various smaller parties attaching themselves to Bell's caravan. The traveling was monotonous and difficult; they suffered torrential rain, treacherous sands, and skin-lacerating winds. Finally, in late February, after two and a half months in the saddle, Bell arrived at the towering gates of Hayyil. It was the end of her pilgrimage and the beginning of her incarceration.

She was given a house in which to stay and was visited by Ibrahim, a court official. She discovered that the Rashid clan's 16-year-old ruler, the amir of Hayyil, was away on a raid and that, in his absence, life in Hayyil had effectively ground to a halt. By this time Bell had virtually run out of money, and no one was willing to redeem a credit note for £200, which had been sold to her by a Rashid agent in Damascus. Even if they had permitted her to leave, she wouldn't have been able to afford to hire men and camels.

As the days passed, she realized that she was effectively under house arrest, forbidden to cross her gates except when called for and then only at night. Hayyil was a city where women were rarely seen or heard. For 10 grueling days, the famous traveler and student of Arab culture sat in her room, waiting to hear when the young emir would return, or if his domineering mother-in-law might allow the *ferengi* to venture out of her house.

Then one night, she was invited to visit the emir's wife, Mudi, in the ancient splendor of the Royal Harem. It was a fascinating encounter that reminded Bell of scenes from *The Arabian Nights*. Mudi

---

PERSIAN INSULTS AND COMPLIMENTS

You son of a burnt father! *(Your father has gone to hell.)*
May you be stung by a Kashan scorpion! *(Scorpions from Kashan were famous for their venomous stings.)*
He puts his cheese in his bottle and rubs his bread on the outside! *(Reference to the proverbial stinginess of the inhabitants of Isfahan.)*
May your shadow never grow smaller! *(Compliment.)*
Kismet! *(It is fate.)*

—AS COMPILED BY ELLA SYKES

---

was a strong, powerful woman, but she had never enjoyed any of the freedoms that Bell took for granted. The two talked for hours.

Soon after, Bell was given her money and allowed to leave Hayyil. She never found out whether her freedom was due to Mudi's intercession or because of some other friendly sheikhs, but she didn't stick around to find out. Bell spent one tense day taking photographs and trying to see the town before departing for Baghdad.

Her return journey was fraught with danger. She avoided an encounter with the Rashid emir, but her party was fired at on several occasions. Instead of maintaining her original intention and carrying on to Riyadh, the capital city of the Sauds, she headed back as quickly as she could to the comparative safety of Baghdad.

Ultimately Bell did not make the journey that she had first intended, but she learned many things that would stand her in good stead in the coming years when she worked as an adviser to the British government. Her doomed relationship with Dick Doughty-Wylie continued to flicker and flame, finally extinguishing when he was killed at Gallipoli in 1915.

1920: Rosita Forbes Reaches Kufara

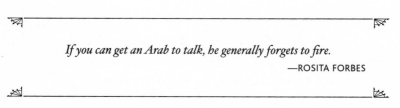

If you can get an Arab to talk, he generally forgets to fire.

—ROSITA FORBES

World War I put a brief halt to geographical exploration for its own sake, but no sooner had it ended than the second great desert explorer appeared. Rosita Forbes was very different from Gertrude Bell. She was no Orientalist or student of Arab culture. She didn't get excited at the sight of a good ruin and wasn't obsessed with ancient history. She did share one quality with all the other "queens of the desert," though: courage. And she had it in spades. Beautiful, ambitious, daring, and always up for an adventure, Rosita Forbes was exploration's "It girl." She was born with three great misfortunes, she wrote: her beauty, her youth, and her gender. Modesty was unlikely to have appeared on the list; as Gertrude Bell put it, "I've never known anyone who can blow their own trumpet so loud as Rosita Forbes."

In 1919, she began her most famous adventure over lunch at Claridge's, where she tried to persuade Ahmed Mohammed Bey Hassanein, an Oxford-educated Egyptian dandy, to assist her on a dangerous expedition to the fabled oasis of Kufara. Several hundred miles from the coast of Libya, in the scorching heart of the Sahara, Kufara was the home of the Senussi, a fundamentalist Islamic sect famous for their hostility toward outsiders. The only previous European to have reached it was the German Gerhard Rohlfs, who lived to tell the tale, but only just. When Bey Hassanein sensibly wavered, Forbes invited him to her home in Norfolk and instructed her family to give his arm a final twist.

For the next six months, Forbes worked hard on creating a credible disguise; she became Khadija, the daughter of a Cirassian slave (well known for their fair skin) and an Arab father. She studied Arabic and the rituals of Islam. Her ambition, she said, was that if she ever had a nightmare, she would cry out in Arabic. She traveled to Europe in search of Emir Feisul, the exiled king of Syria and sharif of Mecca, in order to get his blessing. En route she had an odd but typically Forbesian encounter with a young journalist and political activist by the name of Benito Mussolini. They met on a station platform in Milan. Local baggage handlers were on strike, so the future Duce helped her retrieve her suitcase and then tried to interview her about modern womanhood. After a few hours of flirting, she was off.

In November 1920, Forbes and Bey Hassanein arrived in Libya to begin their final preparations. All the odds were stacked against them: Both the Italian colonial authorities and most of the local Arabs were suspicious, and initially it was impossible to hire camels. To add to their woes, Forbes had twisted her ankle so badly that she could barely walk. They had one ace in their hand, though: a letter that she had charmed out of Sayed Idris es Senussi, the head of the clan, approving their journey. Over the coming months, that letter would serve them well.

In early December, they stole away in the dead of night from Jedabia, the last colonial town. They had two Bedouin guides, two Sudanese soldiers, and minimal provisions. When they later attached themselves to a larger caravan, the hostility between the Bedouin and the North Africans increased worryingly. Over the next two months, Forbes and her men trudged through the desert, stumbling from oasis to oasis, always hungry, always thirsty, always wary of anyone they met in case they proved to be spies or assassins.

The terrain was hostile enough, but the real danger was in the swirl of intrigue that surrounded their party. Many Senussi saw through Forbes's disguise and, official letter or no letter, wished her dead. Some wanted to kill her because she was an infidel, others because of her supposed wealth. Her two principal guides, Yusuf and Mohammed, did have an incentive to help her succeed: They had been warned that if anything happened to Forbes, they would be executed.

Under her Arab dress, Forbes carried two fully loaded Colt revolvers and a prismatic compass. She tried her best to compile a map, but her guides were very suspicious and reluctant to name anything.

The final stage of the journey was the most perilous. In the midst of continued feuding between the Arabs and the Sudanese, Abdullah, another chief guide, "lost his head." As they trekked through the desert, tantalized by mirages, their feet blistered and their throats parched, he flailed around, taking the party first one direction and then another. When their water ran out, Forbes and Bey Hassanein desperately drank the juice from their last tin of carrots; their Bedouin had nothing. After nine days they found a muddy pool, which frantic hands turned into a deep well. They had survived, but as they made their way into Buseima, the last oasis before Kufara, once again their minds turned to the hostile tribesmen around them.

They were now in the land of the Zouia, one of the most feared tribes in the eastern Sahara whose loyalty to the Senussi was by no means guaranteed. As Forbes's party pressed on to Kufara, more rumors circulated of ambushes to come and feuds to be settled. The sand dunes grew bigger and the travel tougher. A splash of white in the distance turned out to be the bleached skeletons of three men.

To make things even worse, Abdullah, the hapless guide, suddenly turned traitor and spread rumors that Forbes and Bey Hassanein were in fact Italians bent on mapmaking and future conquest. Evidently he hoped that if they were killed, no one would know of his incompetence. Bey Hassanein rose to the occasion and spent his time trying to persuade Zouia elders that they could be trusted. Forbes kept her revolvers close and looked forward to a fight; it would be a better end, she thought, than dying of thirst in the desert.

The battle never came. Bey Hassanein's diplomacy prevailed, and he persuaded the Zouia that he and Forbes should be treated as guests rather than enemies. Finally, on January 14, five weeks after they departed Jedabia, they arrived at Kufara. By this time they had begun to doubt if it really existed. Kufara was, in fact, a series of small oases set in a deep wadi surrounded by a ring of steep black hills. Forbes was elated, but not for long. Once again the rumor mill started, and once again their hosts swung from generous hospitality to deep suspicion. They were told that they could see the main towns, but Forbes was warned to keep away from the outlying villages. She took stealthy photographs from cameras hidden in the folds of her robe but was now very careful to cover her face with a veil. She never saw any other women, and even the men seemed hesitant to leave their anonymous, high-walled houses.

After nine fascinating though frustrating days, they set off on the return journey. This time they insisted on traveling light, leaving their Sudanese guards behind and taking only four Bedouin guides. Forbes's plan was to return north via a different route, to confound any potential pursuers. After two days, they discovered that they were indeed being followed. They doused their fires and traveled through the night. The plan worked and they shook off the threat. When they reached the ancient city of Jaghabub, they looked forward to crossing into Egypt, but the desert wasn't going to let them go so easily.

Bey Hassanein fell off his camel and broke his collarbone. He tried to continue, but he was clearly in great pain. Forbes resolved to leave him with two guides and set off in search of help when suddenly, out of the darkness, came an English voice. It was a British Camel Corps Patrol, sent to find them by the British governor of Siwa, just across the border in Egypt. Then came tea and milk, sausages, tomatoes, new camels, tobacco, and a soft pillow for Bey Hassanein's shoulder. They had made it.

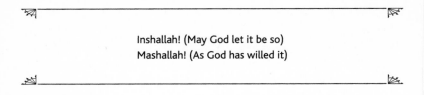

Inshallah! (May God let it be so)
Mashallah! (As God has willed it)

Back in England, Forbes was fêted by the press and showered with honors by all the leading European geographical societies. There were occasional gossipy (but totally unfounded) rumors about her relationship with Bey Hassanein, but most of Europe and America fell over itself to congratulate her. Some journalists, however, were impossible to please: Couldn't she look more like an explorer? she was asked. She was simply too young and too beautiful.

1930: Freya Stark Travels through the Land of the Assassins

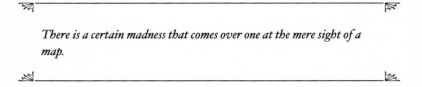

There is a certain madness that comes over one at the mere sight of a map.

The third great desert explorer was the incomparable Freya Stark. She didn't have the grandeur of Gertrude Bell or the penchant for melodrama of Rosita Forbes. Her early expeditions had a picaresque, almost shambolic quality; she traveled with guides who reeked of cheese and resembled village idiots. She fell ill regularly, and her ambitions were often thwarted by officials and sometimes even her own men. She was unlucky in love, full of doubts about her appearance, and for many years lived in the shadow of a domineering mother. And yet for all her insecurities, Freya Stark had a core of steel and was a natural-born traveler.

At the age of 4, Stark ran away from home with a toothbrush and a penny in her pocket, aiming to go to sea; at the age of 89, she trekked through the Himalayas on a donkey. In between, she traveled through Asia and the Middle East, making epic journey after epic journey. By the end of her life, she had published 18 volumes of travel writing, 8 volumes of letters, and 4 volumes of autobiography. Like many great travelers, though, she probably will be best remembered for her first efforts, and in particular her expeditions to the Land of the Assassins.

It started with Stark reading as much as she could about her chosen subject. The Assassins were an obscure eleventh-century sect, who used murder for religious ends. For 200 years they terrorized the Middle East, before they were smashed by the all-conquering Mongols. Their last strongholds were in the Alamut Valley, and it was here that Freya Stark headed in 1930. In searching for traces of the Assassins, she was consciously following in the footsteps of the great historical explorer Marco Polo, who first brought their story to Europe.

Stark's expedition did not start auspiciously: A banking hitch left her with just £2.00 in her pocket to make a potentially long and grueling journey. She begged a lift and hoped for the best. Prior to starting, Stark had not in fact been able to find the castle of Alamut on any map, but her luck turned when she arrived at the small, dusty town of Qasvin. There, by chance, she met a doctor who turned out to be one of the owners of the Rock of Alamut, the remote promontory where the Assassins' castle once stood. For a small fee, he rented her some mules and some men to look after them.

They were a ragtag bunch: Aziz, the leader (who insisted on bringing his mother and his child along for the ride), and two assistants, the tall and imbecilic Ismail and the splendidly christened though equally challenged Refuge of Allah.

Together they trekked higher and higher into the foothills of the Elburz Mountains. Occasionally, local people were hostile and refused to let their children accept Stark's toffees, but most treated her with great hospitality. Along the route she took photographs and corrected the many mistakes she found on her map. No one was worried about giving her information, but everyone seemed to have a different name for geographical features, and some seemed to have several. After 10 days of walking and climbing, the group reached their goal.

The Rock of Alamut was eerie and imposing but something of an anticlimax, especially when Stark discovered that several Europeans had preceded her and that there was even a designated pair of local guides. Still, it was a huge thrill to have reached the Assassins' fortress; Freya Stark was an archetypal historical explorer, and nothing excited her more than to walk through and gaze on historical landscapes.

She was similarly excited to hear reports of another castle, Lamiasar, which no outsider had ever visited. It was said to have a garden, and Stark wondered if it might be the famed secret garden where novice Assassins were plied with hashish before being sent out on their deadly missions.

A year later, she returned to find out. Neither Aziz nor Refuge of Allah was available, so she had to make do with the pungent Ismail and two mules. Together they retraced their steps from the previous year, climbing up into the hills, chatting to local people as they went. Once again, Stark got lucky. She found an old man who knew exactly where the ruins of Lamiasar were. Two days and several old men later, she arrived. There was no sign of the fabled garden of the Assassins, but the ruins were impressive. Stark made detailed notes and was delighted at the thought of more ancient castles in the vicinity, but Ismail wasn't eager to remain in the mosquito-infested valleys that surrounded them. Stark prepared for an argument, but before she could make her case, she suddenly she felt ill with malaria.

She lay desperately ill under a tree, tended by local women until, by another supreme stroke of good fortune, Ismail discovered that an

Iranian doctor was staying at a local village. For the next five weeks he looked after her. Stark was alarmed at his habit of prescribing doses of medicine three times higher than suggested on the box, but there was little doubt that he saved her life. When she recovered, she decided to make an attempt on the Throne of Solomon, the third tallest mountain in Persia, then unconquered. Once again, though, her guide let her down and took her on a route that had no chance of success. Never admitting total defeat, Stark headed to Tehran via the valley of the Shahrud, exploring villages and landscapes that time had forgotten, dependent as ever on the kindness of strangers.

AFRICA

Christina Dodwell
Florence Baker
May French Sheldon
Beryl Markham
Rosita Forbes
Mary Kingsley
Karen Blixen
Stella Court Treatt
Mary Hall
Lady Florence Dixie

Africa was another popular women's destination in the heyday of nineteenth- and twentieth-century exploration. As we will see with the East, many women went there to accompany their diplomat husbands, and as with the desert, tourism came to the region much earlier than many people realize. It is amazing to look, for example, at the women who attempted a land journey from Cape Town to Cairo. You might think that this was a very arduous challenge, yet the first woman to attempt it, in 1905, was Miss Mary Hall, a rather matronly 50-year-old who referred to herself as a "world tourist" and would have guffawed if anyone suggested that she should be called an "explorer." Her motto was "Take every precaution and abandon all fear," and when anyone asked her what she was doing, she simply replied that she was taking a walk. Her little promenades included confrontations with spear-waving tribesmen, eating elephant steaks for dinner, and the occasional game of tennis in the middle of the rain forest.

Taking a walk in the African jungle was intrepid enough for some women, but for others, the real thrill came when they went totally off the beaten track.

1885: Annie Hore Makes a Pioneering Journey through East Africa

Anne Hore was the wife of an English missionary who made a very uncomfortable journey in 1885 in a "bath chair" designed by her husband. It took a team of 16 men to carry it, working in 2-man shifts, and was, as Hore put it, "a most comfortable means of transport—except when in motion." To add to her discomfort, for most of the latter half of the journey, she had to carry her sick young son on her lap. For her husband she was a guinea pig, sent out to prove that staunch English-women could survive, and move around, in darkest Africa, while he and the other male missionaries got on with the important work of saving souls. Hore, however, wasn't happy to play such a passive role; she used the book that she wrote afterward about her journey to make an im-passioned argument against the continued practice of slavery.

1891: May French Sheldon Goes on Safari

Were she a man
We should call her manly,
As it is, there are some who,
In wishing to laud,
Are accustomed to call her the female Stanley

—*PUNCH* MAGAZINE

May French Sheldon is one of the great characters in the history of women's exploration. Small in stature but huge in self-confidence, in 1891 she organized and led an expedition through the East African bush, from Zanzibar to Mount Kilimanjaro. To the Africans she met, she was the self-proclaimed "White Queen"; to audiences back in Eng-land, she was the "female Stanley."

Sheldon was an American who had gone to England in the 1880s with her husband, Eli, a successful investment banker. She dabbled in publishing until one day she met Sir Henry Morton Stanley, the African explorer, and found a new mission in life.

In spite of the opposition of her friends and her husband, whose heart she left "aching with apprehension," she set off alone on a daring safari. En route to Africa, she stopped at Zanzibar, whose sultan was so impressed that he compelled each of his 142 concubines to present her with a ring. However, the European officials she encountered ranged from the discouraging to the downright hostile. At the time, there was a lot of friction between Britain and Germany, which were vying for

influence in the region. Neither country wanted an American woman wandering around on her own in the jungle.

Sheldon ignored them all and set about hiring 138 porters to carry her goods and equipment. "Bebe Bwana" (woman master), as her men called her, played the archetypal white explorer. She traveled in style with a personal masseuse, a portable bath, and a huge wicker palanquin in which she reclined and slept. Around her waist she wore a medicine belt and a pair of fully loaded Colt revolvers; her walking stick carried a flag with the motto *Noli me tangere,* or "Don't cling to me." She would lunch with tremendous pomp and ceremony in order to instruct local people in the ways of white people. Her wardrobe included a platinum wig and a white silk dress from Paris, which she wore during meetings with important chiefs.

En route to her goal, she collected dozens of artifacts and took over 500 impressions of native hands and feet. Unlike most other white explorers, she refused to pay taxes, or *hongo,* to local chiefs, although she did carry an emporium of presents, which she handed out with

HOW TO GET AROUND IN AFRICA: THE PALANQUIN

May French Sheldon commissioned a handmade wicker palanquin for her trek through Africa. It weighed 73 pounds, had yellow curtains, and was fitted out with drawers for medicines and toiletries and a seat that folded out to become a bed. One night Sheldon awoke to hear a strange rustling sound above her head. Gingerly she opened the door and peeked out, only to see a giant python wrapped around the roof of the palanquin. Her men hacked the snake to pieces.

tremendous gravitas. Important personages were given umbrellas, horns, music boxes, and clocks; lesser dignitaries were presented with silver rings with her name inscribed on the inside.

For all her bombast, Sheldon undoubtedly found it very difficult to control such a large group of men and to keep her cool in often difficult circumstances. Her caravan was attacked by lions, pythons, ants, and mosquitoes. When she wasn't urging her men on or dealing with incipient mutinies, she had to minister to numerous illnesses, which ranged from leprosy to the ubiquitous fever. Sheldon survived remarkably unscathed, until she was hit in the face by a branch that left a thorn embedded in her eye. She ignored it, writing that "with one eye I saw more than I can ever hope to recount of the grandeur of Kilimanjaro," but by the end of the journey the experience started to take its toll. Close to Lake Chala, she was dropped into a river by her porters while inside her palanquin. Sheldon survived, but she hurt her back and developed severe dysentery. She spent most of her return journey prostate with fever; she was so ill that when she finally returned to London, her husband's first words were a plaintive "Does she live?"

Sheldon's epic trek made her famous enough to be invited to become one of the first female members of the Royal Geographical Society, but her husband died shortly after she returned and left her with very little money. She tried to set herself up as an authority on all matters African, but she was not taken as seriously by the press as Mary Kingsley, another female African explorer. In 1903, Sheldon returned to Africa at the behest of the Congo Reform Society to investigate the cruel empire of Leopold II. She astonished everyone by reporting that the Belgian king was more benevolent than despotic. Cynics claimed that she had been paid off.

1893: Mary Kingsley Goes Upriver

The patron saint of African explorers has to be Mary Henrietta Kingsley, the Victorian spinster who went to the Congo in search of "fish and fetish" and came back a collector, a committed traveler, and an advocate of native rights. She grew up in the shadow of her brilliant but erratic father, George Kingsley, who spent most of his time abroad and didn't believe that women needed to be educated. He insisted that she master the skill of ironing before she was allowed to learn German. Kingsley spent most of her youth caring for her mother and later for her father, but in between meals and sessions at the ironing board she read widely, following the exploits of British explorers such as Sir Richard Burton and David Livingstone as well as subscribing to *The English Mechanic*. At the age of 31, with her brother in China and her parents in the grave, Kingsley finally tasted freedom.

In 1893 and 1894, she made two journeys to West Africa, traveling through modern-day Congo. She spent much of her time with men

MARY KINGSLEY'S GUIDE TO WEST AFRICAN ANIMALS AND HOW TO DEAL WITH THEM

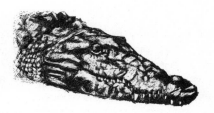

CROCODILES . . .

. . . or "large Silurians," are much more comfortably watched from the deck of a steamer than from the middle of a canoe. During her trips through the mangrove swamps of the Ogunwe River, she frequently encountered their musky smell and on several occasions was severely menaced by crocodiles. The largest specimen she measured (once it was dead, of course), was 22 feet long.

When attacked: Hit them on the head with your paddle and then make for deeper water, where they are not so comfortable.

LEOPARDS . . .

. . . are less common than crocodiles but much more dangerous. During her time in Africa, Mary Kingsley had to break up two fights between leopards and dogs.

When attacked: A well-aimed stool will separate a leopard from its victim, but for a real deterrent, throw a heavy object at its head.

ELEPHANTS . . .

. . . are great for trophy hunters and for those who love boasting about their exploits, but if you, like Mary Kingsley, are not so inclined, then they are best watched from a distance.

If charged: Dodge them around the biggest trees you can find, stay downwind, and when they lose sight and smell of you, lie down for as long as you can.

HIPPOS . . .

. . . are another occupational hazard for anyone bent on exploring the mangrove swamps. Mary Kingsley called them "viscera in big bags" and wondered whether they were God's first or last creations in the animal world.

To avoid close contact: Stay away from "hippo grass" and keep an eye on unusually muddy paths leading down to the river's edge.

SNAKES . . .

. . . are very common in the swamps. The best way to catch them is with a cleft stick. When trying to capture a snake, concentrate on the head, or "the business end," as Mary Kingsley called it. But be careful. Occasionally it is difficult to work out which end is which. The longest (dead) snake that Mary Kingsley measured was a 25-foot boa constrictor.

Culinary tip: Roast snake is far superior to any African fowl.

from the Fan tribe, studying their customs. She was very proud of her mastery of the native canoe but found that she was usually expected to lead her men, wading through swamps and fording rivers, rather than take a more ladylike position at the rear.

At first, the natives feared that she was a temperance campaigner, so she began trading in order to bond with them and to justify her travels. She cut a curious figure in the jungle, maintaining her European clothes and refusing even to contemplate the trouser skirts that some other women wore. Her typical uniform was a long, tight-waisted skirt, a shirt with a high collar, and a small fur cap.

Having been so long trapped at home, Kingsley described herself as feeling like a "boy with a new half-crown." She eulogized the beauty of mangrove forests, comparing the richness of their flora and fauna to a Beethoven symphony and, more directly, comparing their sunsets to a Turner painting.

Kingsley was much more rigorous and methodical in her exploration than May French Sheldon and amassed a considerable collection of artifacts and specimens for the British Museum. She was also much more respectful of the Africans she met and felt a real empathy with them. She once wrote, "Africa is a woman," and elsewhere added that "an African is no more an undeveloped white than a woman is an undeveloped man."

Back in Britain, Kingsley handed over dozens of artifacts and specimens to her scientific friends and wrote a series of very successful books detailing her encounters with crocodiles, cannibals, and witch doctors and discussing the future of Africa. She became an important and respected voice on African affairs and spoke out against both the imposition of property taxes on Britain's colonial subjects and what she saw as overzealous attempts to limit trade in alcohol.

For all the wit of her books and her apparent self-possession, Mary Kingsley was a tormented soul who confessed in a letter to a friend that she had gone to Africa "hoping to die." Indeed, the French colonial authorities were not eager to let her pass through their territory because they thought that she was bent on self-destruction. Her final trip to Africa came in 1899, when she abandoned her exploring ambitions to volunteer as a nurse during the Boer War. She died in the following year and, according to her last wish, was buried at sea.

1909: Charlotte Mansfield Attempts to Travel from Cape Town to Cairo in a Year

In 1909, the romance novelist Charlotte Mansfield set off from Britain on what was billed as the most "venturesome expedition ever undertaken by a woman": a 2,000-mile journey from the Cape Town to Cairo to be completed in a year. She had learned how to take photographs and how to shoot at a rifle range and had equipped herself with all the latest camping equipment. Mansfield made the first part of her journey, from South Africa to modern-day Zimbabwe, by rail and then hired 49 porters to carry her belongings into the swamps of central Africa. At first she waxed lyrical, comparing the atmosphere of a forest camp at night to the interior of the Duomo in Milan, but then her dog died after being bitten by a tsetse fly, and she herself contracted malaria. When Mansfield reached Lake Tanganyika, she learned that the famous geographer Professor Beattie was hot on her trail with the same ambition and so, reluctantly, she gave up. She sold off her remaining supplies and possessions and headed for the coast. Mansfield wasn't quite finished with Africa though; shortly after her trek ended she married Vladimir Raffalovich, a mining engineer based in South Africa.

1924–1926: Stella Court Treatt Drives from Cape Town to Cairo

In 1926, Stella Court Treatt managed to complete the journey that Charlotte Mansfield had abandoned. She was the glamorous wife of Major "C. T." Court Treatt, a chisel-jawed former soldier. He put the idea to his wife while she was in the hospital recovering from an attack of fever, and it was just the tonic she needed. Together with three friends and a journalist from the *Daily Express,* they attempted to drive two Crossley motorcars from South Africa to Egypt, traveling all the way via British territory.

Stella was in charge of one vehicle, and along the route she proved herself to be hardy, fearless, and a lot of fun. A self-confessed tomboy, she dressed in shorts and a shirt and frequently was mistaken for a young man. Though occasionally she longed for cigarettes, chocolate, a big bath, and a silk robe, most of the time she was content with the endless rain, armies of fleas, and a hard seat.

The Court Treatts were the second party to attempt the Cape-to-Cairo motor journey and the first to succeed. The last person to try, another British soldier, Captain Kelsey, had died in the attempt. It was not hard to see why: The first 400 miles almost broke their spirits with endless rain and mud, and the remaining 1,500 miles took them through territory where roads were a luxury.

When the strain got to be too much, Stella berated herself in her diary for being too soft, but for the most part she breezily dismissed any low spirits as "just a reaction" and tried to make the best of any problems. Lions prowling around her tent at night were written off as "an awfully thrilling thrill" while lethal snakes were an opportunity for a "snappy pair of shoes," if she could get a shot in.

The couple's ingenuity was endless—when they couldn't find a bridge or a fording point, they crossed rivers submarine style, plugging up their engines, removing their bags, and then dragging the vehicles across the *bottom* of the riverbed. By the end, they were so well drilled that, after a river crossing, they could have their vehicles back on the road within two and a half hours.

When they reached the Sudan, the natives were amazed to find a little boy who looked like a woman, or so they thought. Stella had deepened her voice and tried to pass herself off as a teenage youth, though she did worry that she might be kidnapped and kept as a museum piece. Finally, after 16 months, the Court Treatts reached their goal and were greeted by huge crowds in Cairo. Stella was slightly worried, however, that after such an epic journey, in which they had had touched and felt "real" things, as she called them, the insincerities of modern life might be hard to put up with.

What, and What Not, to Wear in Africa

It was not until the second half of the twentieth century that trousers became a common item in women's wardrobes; prior to this, many considered them distinctly unladylike. The rules were slightly different for travel, with some women adopting trousers for mountaineering, but there was still a lot of prejudice against women wearing what

was seen as men's clothing. Mary Kingsley was one passionate advocate of skirts. She wrote that she would "rather perish on a public scaffold" than wear "you know what I mean." She claimed that skirts both enabled women travelers to keep up appearances and were practical clothing. When she fell into a hunter's pit full of wooden spikes, Kingsley was saved from injury by the folds of her skirt and thereafter famously proclaimed "the blessings of a good thick skirt."

Other women Victorian travelers also claimed that skirts and dresses were very practical. When the so-called world pilgrim Mary Hall got her dress wet on her epic trek from Cape Town to Cairo, she simply stripped down to her petticoats, confident that her porters wouldn't notice the difference. Modern-day explorer Christina Dodwell is also a fan of the long skirt. A smart skirt is both comfortable in the heat and practical and, according to Dodwell, likely to make a better impression on strangers than jeans or shorts. Her more general tip for remote travel is to dress like a teacher, the epitome of respectability.

THE FAR EAST

The Far East was another powerful lure for women travelers in the nineteenth century. Some went out to accompany their husbands and fathers on military and diplomatic postings; others went independ-

ently, either to hunt or simply to see the sights. Many were attracted to the region because of its rich cultural and religious traditions. Within Europe, there was a lot of interest in Buddhism and Hinduism, but quite a few women also went east as Christian missionaries, hoping to convert the heathens.

Whatever the reasons, the East made a huge impression on everyone who visited it.

1898: Susie Rijnhart Attempts to Reach Lhasa

When it comes to sheer dogged persistence, few people can match the Canadian missionary Susie Rijnhart. In 1898, she attempted to become the first woman to take the word of God to Lhasa, the capital of Tibet. She lost her servants but that didn't stop her; she lost her child but that didn't stop her; she lost her husband and that didn't stop her. Even when she was finally forced out of Tibet, she never lost faith and was soon planning her return.

Susie had arrived in Tibet in 1894 with her Dutch husband Petrus Rijnhart, a Protestant missionary. Initially they settled on the border between China and Tibet, near the famous Kumbum monastery, one of the great centers of Tibetan Buddhism.

Susie was a rather intolerant soul who was constantly railing against the idolatrous practices of local monks. She was also disgusted by the poor hygiene of the Tibetans, who seemed happy to be handle food one moment and dried yak turds the next. Both Rjinharts were very confused by local polytheism: How could anyone be a Taoist, a Buddhist, and a Confucian at the same time? Adding Christianity to the list, however, was much harder than they thought.

Susie and Petrus discovered that it was futile to preach to large crowds of Tibetans, so instead they concentrated on their medical mission. As patients came in, they were sent to waiting rooms adorned with religious images; as they left, they were offered translations of religious tracts.

The Rijnharts compared their mission to that of David Livingstone, and, like the famous Scottish missionary, they made few converts. Nevertheless, they clung on to their ambition to take Christianity to Lhasa. The facts that no European had visited the city for many years and every recent Western attempt had ended in failure or death did not put them off.

In April 1898, they left with two years' worth of food, two servants, a Mongolian monk, and their 18-month-old son, Charlie. The Rijnharts did not think of themselves as explorers — that was far too frivolous an occupation for two modern-day evangelists — but they could not help being fascinated by the landscapes they saw and the people they met.

At first the journey went well, but then, during their crossing of the high Kuenlen Mountains that separate north and south Tibet, their servants suddenly deserted them. Shortly afterward, five of their ponies were stolen. Charlie was able to cope with the high altitude and the harsh traveling conditions, but he was laid low by his first batch of milk teeth. After his eighth tooth came through, he developed a high fever that raged for two days before he died. His parents placed his body in a wooden drug box and hid it under a boulder to keep the bandits and the wolves at bay. Susie Rjinhart wrote in her diary: "The Cold earth of Tibet wraps itself around its first Christian child." Still they soldiered on, only stopping to celebrate their fourth wedding anniversary.

Local nomads were curious but reluctant to help them for fear of retribution by government officials. The closer they got to Lhasa, the more patrols they saw. Finally at the town of Nagch'uk'a, they were ordered to turn back and given a military escort to make sure that they complied. Their guides, however, led them into a trap, deserting them when they encountered a group of heavily armed men. The Rjinhardts were forced to abandon most of their possessions and to continue on their retreat alone.

Eventually, they came to a river and saw a large encampment of yak herders on the other side. Petrus rode off to ask for their help, but he never returned. Susie was like a biblical character, a lost soul in the middle of the wilderness with only her prayer book and her Bible to comfort her.

Nothing before, nothing behind,
The steps of faith
Fall on the seeming void, and find
The rock beneath.
—John Greenleaf Whittier

Somehow she crossed the river herself, but there was no sign of her husband, and before she knew it, the Tibetans had stolen almost all her remaining supplies. She shamed a local chieftain into giving her new guides by warning him that if she carried on alone and died, he would get the blame.

Finally, after months on the trail, she made her way to the Chinese border and pitched up at the nearest mission house. Her first words were "Is Queen Victoria still alive?" It had been an awful journey, but she put her survival down to divine intervention and compared her ordeal to that of the early apostles. A year later, she came back to China with another missionary husband, this time a fellow Canadian. She was soon pregnant, but she died three weeks after giving birth.

1913: Beatrix Bulstrode Tours Mongolia

Beatrix Bulstrode was a British journalist who made a pioneering tour through Mongolia in 1913. Her aim was to find "primitive life amongst primitive people," and in Central Asia she got her wish. She made two journeys, one with local guides and European missionaries and the other with Edward Manico Gull, a fellow traveler who was to become her husband.

Their expedition took them from Peking to Ulan Bator in Mongolia and then all the way across Mongolia to Russia. En route Bulstrode dodged bandits, haggled with horse traders, and attempted to buy Mongolian artifacts. One of the "highlights" of her expedition was a visit to a jail, where she found dozens of inmates incarcerated in tiny coffin-like boxes barely a cubic yard in size; some of them had been there for years. Bulstrode noted that the Chinese prisoners were able to poke their heads out of the sides of their boxes because of their relatively small heads, but the Mongolians were unable to do so because of the large size of their craniums.

Bulstrode was a keen and candid observer of Mongolian life. She noted that most women were treated badly unless they were young and beautiful, in which case they had a great life. She also noticed that Mongolians did not bury their dead, preferring to leave them to rot on the outskirts of town. One of Bulstrode's hobbies was phrenology, and once she made the unfortunate mistake of collecting a skull, which, on

YURT ETIQUETTE

OR HOW TO MAKE A GOOD IMPRESSION IN A MONGOLIAN TENT

1. Shout "Nuhoi," Mongolian for "dogs," as you approach a tent. This should bring out the owners of any canines in the vicinity; by law they are required to control their animals.
2. Never take a whip or a riding crop inside a yurt, as this would be seen as an act of aggression.
3. Never sit with your feet facing the back of the yurt. This is very bad manners.
4. Headgear is usually left on, but if you have to remove it, then it must be placed higher up than your seating position.
5. Snuff should be presented first to your host and then to the other guests before you partake yourself.

—As compiled by Beatrix Bulstrode

closer inspection, turned out to be full of rotting brains. She was too squeamish to clean it out and no one in her party was willing to touch it, so Bulstrode had to stage a road accident to get rid of what had been her prize specimen.

Her most embarrassing moment came when she jokingly held out a cigarette to a Mongolian toddler, only for the lad to take up her offer and wander back to his yurt to smoke it.

1924: *Alexandra David-Néel Becomes the First European Woman to Reach Lhasa*

Frenchwoman Alexandra David-Néel was probably the best-known woman traveler of the 1920s and was most famous for her expedition to Lhasa in 1924. She succeeded where Susie Rjinhardt had failed, because she was a much more empathetic traveler who was able to adopt a very convincing disguise.

For many years, David-Néel had studied Tibetan Buddhism, and she was well versed in the customs and language of Tibet. If she revealed herself to be a *Mig kar,* a white-eyed European, she knew that she would be thrown out of Tibet straightaway. So she assumed the role

of an *arjopa,* a Buddhist pilgrim on the road to Lhasa, traveling with a Tibetan companion, Yongden. At first they walked at night and slept during the day, but David-Néel worried that it made them look more suspicious, so they reverted to normal hours and reconciled themselves to meeting fellow pilgrims.

David-Néel's basic disguise was simple but effective. She wore typical peasant clothing with a belt wrapped around her head for a hat; concealed inside the folds of her dress she carried a gun, a compass, and some money. To round off her disguise, she darkened her skin with a mixture of charcoal and cocoa powder. As the journey continued and she became dirtier and dirtier, the illusion deepened. She wore her hair in long braids with yak hair extensions, as was the custom of Ladakh, her fictitious homeland. When she found a greasy fur bonnet by the wayside, her disguise was complete: Yongden told her leave it where it was, saying that it was bad luck to pick up an abandoned hat, but David-Néel was convinced that it was a gift from the gods.

On a few occasions, her cover slipped. Once, when she was eating stew with her fingers, the cocoa and charcoal came off, revealing her white skin, but fortunately no one noticed. She also had a few scary moments when doing the washing up, but her luck held.

If her makeup was a little unreliable, the second element of David-Néel's disguise—her Tibetan traveling companion and adopted son, Yongden—was much more secure. They had met many years earlier at a monastery in Sikkim and became lifelong friends. Yongden invariably ate and spoke first, thus shielding David-Néel from strangers; while he feasted, David-Néel fasted. While he was fêted, she faded into the background and let him take center stage.

It was not always easy playing pilgrims. They had plenty of money to buy provisions, but they rarely used it, for fear of giving themselves away. Instead they had to beg for food and take whatever they got, even if this meant dirty crusts of bread or rancid animal innards. David-Néel had to carry out "intimate personal tasks" in public, and, to make her disguise more convincing, she adopted Tibetan gestures, such as blowing her nose between her fingers.

At one point, though, things almost fell apart. It was nighttime, Yongden was away, and David-Néel was sitting alone in camp, cooking

HOW TO KEEP WARM IN THE COLD

Alexandra David-Néel was a notable exponent of the ancient art of *tumo* breathing, an arcane technique to literally think yourself warm. It was a useful skill in Tibet, a country where it could get so cold that people were not embarrassed to warm themselves over funeral pyres.

In her writing, David-Néel stressed that *tumo* was a secret practice handed down from Buddhist lamas to their students, but she did reveal its basics:

1. Go to an isolated place.
2. Clear your nostrils.
3. Whilst breathing out, think about banishing pride, anger, jealousy and sloth.
4. On an in-breath try to draw in the spirit of Buddha.
5. Breathe slowly and deeply, like a bellows.
6. Visualize flames emanating from your solar plexus

David-Néel wrote that in order to practice their *tumo* breathing, it was traditional for monks to sit by a lake or river draped in a wet blanket and attempt to dry themselves by thought alone. On her own trip through Tibet in 1924, David-Néel and Yongden found themselves in desperate straits on a damp, wet mountainside where it was impossible to get a fire going. Using *tumo* breathing, David-Néel managed to dry a bundle of moss that she held close to her skin, then used the moss to start a fire.

a simple meal. Suddenly a man dressed like a hermit wandered out of the woods and sat down at her fire. He demanded food and then, looking her in the eye, asked her why she was traveling in disguise. She did not recognize him, but he claimed to have seen her at a monastery many years earlier. This very awkward moment ended when the hermit melted away into the shadows, leaving David-Néel wondering whether he had been real or a wandering spirit.

When they finally got to Lhasa, David-Néel found herself tested again when she was forced to take her hat off at a temple. Underneath was a mass of unwashed hair, with very obvious extensions of a different color. Fortunately, the Tibetans around her did not pay too much attention, evidently thinking, as she hoped they would, that it was the fashion of her adopted homeland.

David-Néel had a good sense of humor and was unflappable. When one day she noticed that a policeman in a Lhasa market was studying her suspiciously, she concocted a ridiculous argument with a stall holder, trying to haggle him down to an unrealistically low price, in order to be seen to be behaving like a bona fide country woman. A few days later, another policeman rudely pushed her out of the way and then hit her with his truncheon. Instead of getting angry, she felt triumphant: Now she really had been accepted as a poor peasant.

After several weeks, David-Néel left Lhasa, fearing that she was about to be called to the local court as a witness in a domestic dispute that she had witnessed. For the return journey, deemed to be much safer, David-Néel changed her disguise and moved a few rungs up the social ladder. She became a rich woman, traveling back through Tibet buying paintings and scrolls. When she finally reached British India, she gave the famous Tibetan salute, *Lha gyalo* (the gods have won), and made straight for the nearest British official to proclaim her victory.

1932: Ella Maillart Makes an Epic Journey through Turkestan and the Celestial Mountains

Ella Maillart was an instinctive nomad who spent most of her life traveling. In her youth, she enjoyed the life of a romantic vagabond, working variously as a model, actress, deckhand, stunt woman, and ski instructor. In the 1930s, she settled down to relentless travel, which she funded through writing and later acting as a tour guide. She is most famous for two epic trips through central Asia, riding overland from India to China in 1934 with the British journalist Peter Fleming (see chapter 4) and a solo journey made two years earlier through Soviet Turkestan.

It wasn't easy for a foreigner to get permission to travel through Russia in the early 1930s, but Maillart was so persistent and optimistic that she managed to cut through all the red tape and attach herself to a group of Russian mountaineers who were attempting to reach the Celestial Mountains of Kyrgyzstan. They were a tough bunch, but Maillart easily matched them in hardiness, making a solo ascent of the 16,400-foot Sari Tor using a pair of ancient skis, which she waxed with roofing tar.

Her climbing companions turned back after the Celestial Mountains, but Maillart carried on. It was a wild country where the men trained eagles for hunting and the women brushed the floors of their tents with bird wings. Maillart felt a great empathy with the Kyrgyzs and Kazaks and had no time for the Soviet shock brigades sent east to revolutionize agriculture, "reform" Muslim society, and force the nomads into permanent settlements.

In Tashkent, she stayed in a Soviet workers' hostel, but whenever possible she tried to lodge with local people. She spent one of her happiest periods at a madrassa in Samarkand, and had a lucky escape when she was invited to spend a night at a house in a local village. Though her hosts were very welcoming, the man of the house, Mustapha, was ill in bed. When Maillart inquired what was wrong with him, they told her that he was recovering from a bout of "tiffy" (typhoid). Maillart made a swift exit.

While in the Celestial Mountains, Maillart glimpsed the huge Takla Makan Desert shimmering in the distance, over the border in China. She longed to go there but didn't have a visa, and knew that if she were caught without one, she would be imprisoned immediately. Two years later she finally got her chance to explore Chinese Turkestan, but that is another story. . . .

WHY YOU SHOULD LEARN TO LOVE LICE

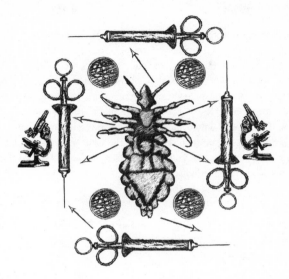

Lice are by no means unique to the East and have accompanied and irritated women explorers all around the world. Unlike fleas, they cannot be transmitted via animals and almost always require physical contact with human carriers, or their bedding or clothing. Three different types of lice are commonly found on humans: body lice, hair lice, and pubic lice (crabs). None is easy to get rid of, because they all have such a high rate of reproduction. A female head louse lives for about a month and lays 7 to 10 eggs a day; pubic lice are not quite so prolific, laying roughly 3 eggs per day. Though few travelers would claim to be a friend of the much-maligned louse, there is more to it than meets the eye.

When missionary Annie Taylor set up her base on the Chinese border in the early 1880s, she noted that Tibetan women were quite proud of their lice because they were said to bring good luck. When they got too numerous, lice made a tasty snack, but a lot of peasants were wary of killing them, fearing that they might be the reincarnation of a dead relative.

When Alexandra David-Néel traveled in disguise through Tibet in 1924, she carried an automatic pistol under her dress. When she had to move the gun, to hide its telltale bulge, she would pretend to be scratching and picking at her lice, a gesture, she knew, that no one would find suspicious.

The most extraordinary louse tale comes from Ella Maillart. When she and the British journalist Peter Fleming decided to make an overland journey from Peking to India, she insisted that they should both be inoculated against typhus. In those days, the vaccine was produced at a laboratory in Peking by deliberately infecting lice and then dissecting their intestines. Roughly 200 lice were needed to produce one dose. The lice were farmed on human volunteers who allowed them to spend half an hour a day grazing on their skin. Often the volunteers were Chinese beggars who were happy to be paid for nursing the parasites that they would probably have carried anyway.

1939: Ursula Graham Bower Is Crowned Naga Queen

It is one thing to go East to study local religion and quite another to be declared a living god. Such was the fate of the British explorer and anthropologist Ursula Graham Bower.

Age 24, Bower had headed for India looking for adventure. She found the colonial set predictable and dull, but when she trekked into the mountains above Manipur and encountered the people of the Naga tribe, in her own words, her "life was changed."

They were equally impressed with her, declaring that Bower was the reincarnation of a Naga god come back to fulfill the prophesy that one day a great leader would arrive who would help them throw the British off their land. The fact that their divine savior was herself British seems rather contradictory, but in such matters Western logic is not always the best guide.

Being a god had its upsides and its downsides. She was given a lot of presents and treated with great respect, but she also found that she had no privacy. Bower's home was constantly invaded by devotees, eager to worship and request blessings. Her divine status was

TIPS FOR DEALING WITH ASIAN FOOD

When she was about to embark on an expedition through Japan in the 1870s, Isabella Bird remarked that apart from general injunctions against making any journey, the most common advice given to her was about food. Everyone from foreign ministers to missionaries seemed to have very strong feelings about what she should and should not eat. For her part, Bird traveled through Japan eating local food, backed up with a supply of beef extract, raisins, chocolate, and brandy. She balked at eating raw fish, though, and was appalled at the speed with which peasants ate their food.

The "food question" is one that comes up on any continent. Asian cuisine is no more different from Western food than African or Inuit food, but it is one subject that a lot of travelers have written about.

SOME ADVICE REGARDING FOOD

IF YOUR HUSBAND APPEARS TO HAVE A WICKED GRIN
ON HIS FACE IN THE MORNING, BE CAREFUL WHAT HE
OFFERS YOU FOR BREAKFAST

Mrs. John Henry Gray was the wife of an Anglican archdeacon who resided briefly in Canton in the late nineteenth century. Her husband was determined that, one way or another, she should taste the local delicacies, namely dog, cat, and rat. He didn't succeed with the last two, but one morning he managed to successfully slip some minced dog into her breakfast. Afterward, she admitted that she found it surprisingly agreeable, especially when combined with potatoes.

LEARN TO LOVE BUTTERED TEA

Break a piece of brick tea and put it into a pot of boiling water.
After twenty minutes, add a large lump of yak butter, rancid or fresh.
Drink as it is, or add tsampa, the coarse meal made from barley.
Slurp like a soup or add sufficient tsampa to make a dough ball.

—Alexandra David-Neel's recipe for buttered tea

EAT LIKE A CAMEL

For Ella Maillart, the most important thing about food was that there was
some. Having gone hungry on too many previous expeditions, when she
journeyed through Turkestan in 1932, she made sure to eat as much as
possible whenever food was available, anticipating that in the future it
might not be. Her friends joked that she was eating enough for four people, but Maillart was unabashed.

_____

not permanent, however. When the Naga elder who had spread the
original rumor of her divinity died, Bower's status declined.

Nevertheless, Bower did fulfill the prophecy in another way. When
in 1943, Japanese forces came close to invading India via Burma, she
organized a guerrilla force of Naga warriors to harass and spy on them.
Her fame as the Naga queen eventually brought a British soldier, Lieutenant Colonel Tim Betts, to visit her in 1945; before long they were
married.

MOUNTAINS

When I reached the Grand Plateau I could not walk any longer. I felt very ill, and I lay down on the snow. I panted like a chicken in the heat. They held me up by my arms on each side and dragged me along. But at the Rochers-Rouge I could get no further, and I said to them "Chuck me into a crevasse and go on yourselves." "You must go to the top," answered the guides. They seized hold of me, they dragged me, they pushed me, they carried me, and at last we arrived. Once at the summit, I could see nothing clearly, I could not breathe, I could not speak.

—MARIA PARADIS, THE FIRST WOMAN TO CLIMB MONT BLANC

Reading Maria Paradis's account of her ascent of Mt. Blanc, it is difficult to see why anyone would want to take up mountaineering. The idea of "panting like a chicken" does not have a particularly heroic ring to it. Nevertheless, Paradis got to top, lived to tell the tale, and profited from her celebrity. She owned a food stall at the foot of Mt. Blanc, catering to the tourists who came every year to gape at Europe's highest mountain. Her fame as the first woman to climb Mt. Blanc kept the cash register ringing, and even today there are streets named after her in her hometown of Chamonix, France.

Initially at least, mountaineering was publicized as a very masculine activity, but the reality was somewhat different. Although they sometimes faced prejudice and occasionally downright hostility, from the early days, there were plenty of enthusiastic women climbers.

1838: Henriette d'Angeville Becomes the First Lady to Climb Mt. Blanc

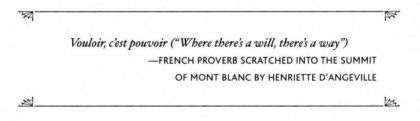

Vouloir, c'est pouvoir ("Where there's a will, there's a way")
—FRENCH PROVERB SCRATCHED INTO THE SUMMIT
OF MONT BLANC BY HENRIETTE D'ANGEVILLE

Henriette d'Angeville, the second woman to climb Mt. Blanc and first to do it under her own steam, was an aristocrat through and through. Her grandfather had been guillotined during the French Revolution and her father was thrown into prison. On his release, he moved the family to a castle near Geneva, where Henriette grew up, surrounded by mountains. It wasn't until she reached the tender age of 44, however, that she finally decided to become the first "lady" to climb Mt. Blanc. Warning her servants to tell any visitors that she was simply "not at home," she traveled to Chamonix, at the foot of the mountain. There, she assembled, dressed, and victualed a small army of porters before heading for the summit.

Two legs of mutton, 2 loins of veal, 24 roast chickens, 3 kilos of chocolate, and a barrel of red wine . . . today her provisions look absurd, but in 1838 it was par for the course. Her clothing was equally extravagant, but, in an era before Gore-Tex and polyester fleece, the only way to guarantee keeping warm was to pile layer upon layer, even if that meant, in d'Angeville's case, wearing 14 pounds of clothing.

Silk stockings
Wool stockings
A foulard cravat
Flannel lined tweed trousers
Various English flannel items worn next to the skin
A blouse made with six layers of wool
A fur-lined bonnet
A velvet mask and a veil to combat the sun
Green spectacles
A tweed shawl
A large straw hat
A fur-lined cloak
Nailed boots
Knitted gloves
Fur gloves
A boa
Thick wool gloves

Local men placed bets as to how quickly she would admit defeat, but d'Angeville was not for turning. She paraded through Chamonix, defiantly sporting her tweed trousers, daring anyone to comment. Then, at the crack of dawn on September 3, 1838, she set off.

It took d'Angeville and her party two days to get to the top. En route, she suffered from headaches, chafed skin, frostbite, heart palpitations, and nausea, but she wouldn't give up. Finally she reached summit and allowed her porters to raise her up on their hands, so that she could claim to have been higher than anyone else before her. She drank a toast to the Comte de Paris, released a carrier pigeon to send back the news of her triumph, permitted her porters to kiss her, and then headed swiftly home.

1871: Lucy Walker Climbs the Matterhorn

No glacier can baffle, no precipice balk her,
No peak can rise above her however sublime
Give three times three cheers for the intrepid Miss Walker
I say my boys, doesn't she know how to climb

—*PUNCH* MAGAZINE

Britain's Lucy Walker was the archetypal Victorian woman climber: a croquet-playing Liverpudlian gentlewoman who, when she wasn't charming the living rooms of polite society, was high up on a mountain, modestly performing some heroic feat. She was the only woman to feature in Edward Whymper's famous engraving *The Club-Room at Zermatt,* a who's who of Victorian mountaineering.

Walker's exploits spanned 21 years, during which time she held many records for first ascents by a woman. She was modest, witty, and determinedly eccentric. Her usual climbing gear was a floral print dress, and her preferred mountain food was sponge cake and champagne—or Asti Spumante when champagne was not available.

Like many Victorian women, Walker first visited the Alps on a family holiday. Her father, Frank, and her younger brother, Horace, were both keen climbers and early members of Britain's Alpine Club. After Lucy's first crossing of an alpine pass in 1858 she was hooked, both to the mountains and to her favorite Swiss guide, Melchior Anderegg.

Together they made over 90 ascents. Walker's most famous achievement was her ascent of the Matterhorn in 1871, just six years after Whymper's epic climb. She scrambled her way to the top in front of her archrival, Meta Brevoort (an American exile who was famous for making most of her ascents in the company of a small dog, Tschingel, who, incidentally, was allowed to join the Alpine Club many years before Meta or Walker). Walker climbed for almost two decades and had an unrivaled record before she retired into genteel obscurity. Three cheers for Lucy Walker!

How to Look Good at High Altitude

What and What Not to Wear
In the nineteenth century, mountaineering clothing was a vexed issue. Even if it was obvious that trousers were far more suitable for climbing than skirts, there were powerful social pressures on women to stick to traditional female attire. A few eccentrics, like Henriette d'Angeville, were willing to scandalize the world with their tweed knickerbockers, but most women put up with skirts for the sake of social propriety. Even as late as the 1930s, authoritative climbing books, such as Geoffrey Winthrop Brown's *Mountain Craft,* were advising women that skirts were "a necessity in the Alps."

The length, style, and permanence of the skirt, however, could be negotiated. In 1859, Mrs. H. W. Cole, one of the earliest female mountaineers to get into print, advised her readers that they should wear a dress made from alpaca or some easy-drying material, which could then be adapted for mountaineering: "Small rings should be sewn inside the seam of the dress, and a cord passed through them, the ends of which should be knotted together in such a way that the whole dress may be drawn up at a moment's notice to the required height."

A simpler solution was to wear a skirt in town, with trousers hidden underneath, and then discard it at the foot of the mountain—though this was not without its dangers. One day, Mrs. Aubrey Le Blond, the first president of the Women's Alpine Club, decided to attempt the Zinal Rothorn in the Alps. She made it to the top and was returning to Chamonix triumphant when she realized that she had left her skirt high up on the mountain. Rather than face the ignominy of arriving in Chamonix skirtless, she and her guide went all the way back up to retrieve it.

Your Skin

Mountaineering, and indeed most forms of exploration, may be good for the soul, but they are rarely good for the skin. Henriette d'Angeville took a small looking glass on her ascent of Mt. Blanc in 1838, but she insisted that it was for practical purposes only, a vital tool that enabled her to apply cucumber pomade correctly to her skin.

Make no mistake: Mountaineering in particular is bad for your complexion. Your skin is alternately frozen, burned, lashed by snow, blasted by wind, soaked by rain, dried, heated, and starved of nourishment. When Mrs. Aubrey Le Blond first took to climbing in the Alps in the 1870s, her great-aunt was furious: "Stop her! She is scandalizing all London and looks like a Red Indian!"

Geoffrey Winthrop Young again offered a novel treatment for sunburn in *Mountain Craft:* Immediately after the incident, bathe the affected skin in very hot water and then cover with it grease. It sounds as excruciating as it does misguided.

Another patent treatment for sunburn was suggested by Lillias Campbell Davidson in her *Hints to Lady Travellers at Home and Abroad* (1889): She advised sunburned women to coat their faces at night with sour cream. This might have been marginally less painful than the hot water treatment, but it was no more efficacious.

It is probably true that women take more care of their appearance than men on expeditions, but the story of the woman climber who spends her idle moments applying lipstick is as much of a myth as it sounds. Nevertheless, it is a surprisingly resilient one.

When in 1955 three members of the Scottish Ladies Climbing Club made the first all-woman expedition to the Himalayas, Indian newspapers were full of stories of knapsacks packed with cosmetics and lipstick being applied at high altitude. The reality was very different. The Scottish women did wash regularly on the way into the mountains, but once they got there, they decided that since they were in a clean world, washing was unnecessary. In order to protect themselves from the sun and the high concentrations of ultraviolet light at altitude, they coated their faces with glacier cream, but they got burned on the inside of their lips when the cream came off.

The press interest in the Scottish women did have one upside: When they returned from their expedition, they were offered free facials at a Bombay beauty salon by a beautician who had seen press photographs of their ravaged faces (and undoubtedly was looking for some free publicity herself).

1908: Annie Smith Peck Climbs Huascarán

Annie Smith Peck was a feisty American with a never-say-die attitude and unbelievable energy. After grabbing an education in the face of parental opposition, she became the first woman college professor in America and looked certain to have a distinguished academic career, until she fell in love with mountaineering.

She made her first major ascent at the age of 45 and gained her place in mountaineering history after a series of expeditions to South America in order to climb Mount Huascarán or, as she called it, "the Apex of America." Peck had her flaws: She was a poor judge of character, a chaotic organizer, and an occasional whiner, and she had appalling dress sense. But she was a model of grit and determination. Even at the age of 85 she was still so enthused by travel and adventure that she embarked on a grueling around-the-world tour.

The sad fact, though, was that Peck's means never matched her climbing ambitions. She made six attempts on Mount Huascarán, and each time she seemed to have less money. On a couple of occasions she did manage to sell her story to the press, but she never had quite enough cash. Her financial problems forced her to make compromises, such as taking madmen along on her expeditions.

It happened on her third attempt Huascarán in 1906. She was so desperate for an assistant that she hired a local man, nicknamed "El Loco." He spoke reasonable English, claimed to have some experience of mountaineering, and, after all, she told herself, he didn't seem *that* bad. Unfortunately, he was. On the mountain, he proved himself to be an incompetent climber and an insubordinate colleague, scampering off before the expedition had ended. Strangely nonchalant, however, Peck took El Loco along on her next attempt! If anything, this time his behavior was even worse. He was cowardly and lazy, he lost Peck's invaluable barometer (without which she couldn't properly measure her altitude), and he encouraged her porters to strike for more money. And, once again, he ignored her orders and retreated when the going got tough. Later, Peck heard that El Loco had been committed to an asylum.

Finally, in 1908, on her sixth attempt, Peck reached the summit of Huascarán and triumphantly claimed a new women's altitude record. It was at this point that she came up against her nemesis: Fanny Bullock Workman.

1913: Fanny Bullock Workman Makes the First Ascent of Nun Kun

Fanny Bullock Workman was an iron-willed, fiercely determined, and hugely effective American explorer who arguably was one of the most important mountaineers of the early twentieth century. Unlike Annie Smith Peck, she was a model of organization and efficiency, a woman who knew what she wanted and knew how to get it.

However, Workman rarely gets enthusiastic write-ups and has never had a proper biography. Why? It sounds trivial, but perhaps there was just something about her name: Fanny Bullock Workman, a strange, heavy, slightly unwieldy combination, a name that even Tristam Shandy

might have pitied. Or perhaps it was her face, which perfectly matched her name; in publicity photographs, she always seemed to be out-staring the camera, grim and determined.

Like Lucy Walker, Fanny Bullock Workman initially took to travel for medical reasons. In Workman's case, though, it was her husband, William Workman, whose health was in need of repair. She was the daughter of a rich American family, and he was a successful doctor burdened with delicate lungs; together they became an awesome team.

Initially the Workmans preferred wheels to crampons, touring the world on that most modern invention, the "safety" bike. Between 1889 and 1902, they rode through Africa, Spain, India, and Burma, to name but a few destinations. Unlike Peck, Fanny Workman had plenty of money to finance her ambitions.

When the Workmans took up mountaineering, they did so with characteristic gusto. William and Fanny spent most of their 30s and 40s climbing and surveying the unmapped regions of the Himalayas and the Karakoram mountains and then writing up their exploits in huge, weighty tomes.

Fanny Workman was a famously tough and uncompromising advocate of women's rights. She was photographed on top of one pass in the Karakoram holding a placard calling for "Votes for Women." She was equally uncompromising when she heard that Annie Smith Peck was claiming a new world record for the ascent of Huascarán. If the story was true, then Workman's own world altitude record was worthless. *If* the story was true.

FANNY VERSUS ANNIE

THE BATTLE FOR THE WOMEN'S ALTITUDE RECORD

When American newspapers heard about Annie Smith Peck's ascent of Huascarán, she was instantly proclaimed "the Queen of the Mountains" and fêted as the world's greatest female climber. Fanny Bullock Workman wasn't so sure. She didn't doubt that Peck had reached the summit, but she was very dubious about the real height of Huascarán. She published her misgivings in *Scientific American* and announced that she had personally commissioned a team of Parisian surveyors to go out and measure the mountain once and for all. Peck was nervous and resented the controversy; throughout her climbing career, she had always been short of funds, and now a fellow mountaineer was about to spend a huge sum of money to destroy her claim to fame. The surveyors returned and announced that Huascarán was 21,800 feet high, not 24,000 feet as Peck had claimed. To add insult to injury, they claimed that she hadn't even climbed to its highest point. (Huascarán has a second northern peak that is 400 feet higher than the southern summit.) Peck argued that the measurement discrepancy wasn't her fault: Local people had told her the height of the mountain because she hadn't been able to take proper barometric measurements. She, in turn, demanded independent proof of Workman's mountaineering record. Peck knew that she was beaten, though; her only comfort was that it had cost the Workmans $13,000 to refute her claim, $10,000 more than it had cost her to climb Huascarán.

1929: Miriam O'Brien Makes the First Ascent of the Grépon

Miriam O'Brien was another American climber who played a crucial role in the history of women's mountaineering. Her stomping ground was the Alps, and her principal claim to fame was her invention of "man-less" climbing, or, to use its rather more poetic French name, *la cordée féminine.* Traditionally, most alpine climbing had been done with the assistance of local guides, who were invariably men, but by the beginning of the twentieth century, experienced mountaineers were increasingly climbing by themselves. Women, however, were always accompanied by guides or male companions until the late 1920s, when Miriam O'Brien decided that it was time for a change.

In 1929, she and Alice Damesme made a famous ascent of the Grépon, a very difficult peak of the Mt. Blanc Massif, *tout seules.* One very testy French climber, Etienne Bruhl, was so incensed by their success that he declared, "Now that it has been done by two women, no self respecting man can undertake it." O'Brien carried on climbing, but after tying the knot with another U.S. climber, Robert Underhill, the remainder of her climbing was done on a "cordee *mariee.*"

Women and Altitude

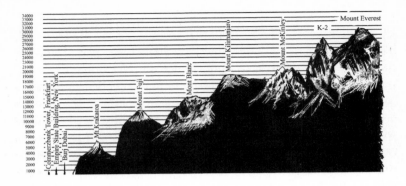

Fifty years ago, one of the common arguments against women taking part in mountaineering expeditions was that they couldn't cope as well as men with high altitude. Today, with thousands of women climbing big mountains every year, it is clear that women can and do cope, but how do they compare?

Research into long-term effects on women has shown that exposure to high altitude reduces life expectancy and increases the rate of aging. It also affects pregnancy: Babies born at high altitude are generally smaller than babies born at sea level. This effect is reduced over time: In Tibet, for example, children born to native Tibetans are relatively bigger than children born to Han Chinese immigrants, whose families have only lived in Tibet for a couple of generations.

Short-term exposure to high altitude—going on an expedition, for example—affects men and women slightly differently. Both genders have to deal with the same basic problem: namely, the higher you climb, the lower the air pressure and the lower the amount of oxygen in the atmosphere. Oxygen starvation is a serious issue; it is possible to operate in an oxygen-poor environment for a certain amount of time, but not without deterioration in physical and mental performance.

The most serious risk for mountaineers at high altitude is of developing edema, a condition in which liquid collects most commonly in the lungs (pulmonary edema) or on the brain (cerebral edema). It is not quite clear what causes edema, but it seems to be related to the effect of low air pressure on the basic cell structure of the body.

Whatever the exact cause, if untreated, cerebral and pulmonary edema can be deadly. Research has shown that women and men show little difference when it comes to cerebral edema, but women are slightly less prone to pulmonary edema than men. They are, however, more susceptible to less serious, peripheral edemas—in the retina, for example.

Pregnant women increase the risks of birth problems when climbing at high altitude, and women climbers using high-estrogen contraceptives run a greater risk of developing thrombosis. Overall, though, there is little evidence that most women climbers they are less able to adapt than men, and if anything they cope better.

How a Woman Climber Can Earn Big Bucks on American TV

In the late 1970s, the American climber Lynn Hill pocketed a check for $4,000 from ABC's television show *That's Incredible!* for an aerial traverse of the *outside* of a hot-air balloon, 6,000 feet up. As the TV helicopters circled around her, she climbed out of the basket and made her way up to the apex of the balloon using a flimsy rope ladder that she had constructed herself. Hill packed a reserve parachute, just in case.

THE POLAR REGIONS

The first man to set foot on Antarctica was Jules Dumont d'Urville, a naval officer who was sent on a mission to claim the geographic South Pole for France. On January 21, 1840, he and his crew made landfall at 66° south, raised the French flag, and named their discovery Pointe Géologie. It was far from the South Pole, but this was a very important moment for the Antarctic. It wasn't until almost a century later that the first woman set foot on Antarctica; in the meantime, the South Pole had been reached by both sled and plane. It was a similar story in the north; until relatively recently, the only women to travel widely in the Arctic were native Inuit (sometimes known as Eskimo).

Why did women stay away from the polar regions for so long? Because they were uncomfortable with the cold? Actually, if anything, women are slightly better equipped than men to cope with low temperatures because of the higher concentration of fat in their bodies. Or was it because they couldn't cope with the darkness of the polar winter? Women are more commonly afflicted with seasonal affective disorder than men, but again, this is not the real cause.

The simple fact is that it is very expensive to get to the polar regions, particularly Antarctica, and money has always been a key factor in any type of exploration. Robert Falcon Scott and Roald Amundsen may be remembered for their heroic endurance on their expeditions to the South Pole, but both had to put equally heroic efforts into raising money to make it all happen.

Until relatively recently, the only woman to engage in any serious polar exploration was the American Louise Arner Boyd, who instigated several expeditions in the 1930s. She was able to do so only because of her large private fortune. In 1950s, the Soviets began sending women to their Antarctic research bases, but there were no American or British women in the Antarctic until the late 1960s.

In the last two decades, things have changed significantly. Modern-day adventurers such as Ann Bancroft, Caroline Hamilton, and Pam Flowers have made daring trips through the polar regions, and the large scientific bases on Antarctica are now home to dozens of women scientists.

1890: Kate Marsden Takes a Train to Siberia

Kate Marsden was an eccentric English nurse who had been blooded in the Russian-Turkish war of the late 1870s. A decade later, she conceived a plan to travel to the wilds of Siberia in search of an herb that was supposed to cure leprosy. Initially she was a very good self-publicist, and managed to engage the support of Queen Victoria and the Empress of Russia. When it came to winter clothing, Marsden took no chances. Her outfit included:

Wool Jaeger underwear
A flannel lined "body"
A thickly wadded eider-down Ulster shawl
A sheepskin that reached all the way to her feet
A reindeer-skin coat
Jaeger stockings
Gentleman's hunting stockings
Pair of knee high felt boots
Brown felt valenkies (boots)
Et ceteras consisting of further shawls, rugs, wraps

When she left the train at Zlatoust in Russia, she discovered that with all her clothes on, she was so bulky that she couldn't climb up onto a sled by herself. It took the combined efforts of three Russian policemen to finally get her aboard. Even for a battle-hardened veteran like Marsden, the journey was physically exhausting; she described herself as feeling "more like a battered old mahogany log than a gently nurtured Englishwoman" after enduring a particularly grueling day. For the final stage, in Siberia itself, she switched from sled to horse and was very embarrassed to find that there was no sidesaddle available. Ultimately, she didn't discover any magic herbs, and the lepers she met were in a terrible state. So she changed tack and campaigned to raise money to build a leper colony. However, at this point, she fell severely out of favor with the Russian government, which was embarrassed by her claims. An official committee was convened to investigate Marsden's journey. Their report stated that the few lepers found in Siberia were in fact treated very well by the imperial government and that she had made up much of her story. So much for trying to do good.

1891: Josephine Peary Heads for Greenland

American Josephine Diebitsch Peary was an extraordinary woman who led an extraordinary life. She was married at the age of 25 to Robert Peary, an obsessively ambitious officer in the U.S. Navy, who was determined to become the foremost Arctic explorer of his day. Although she fell head over heels, he was less romantic, confiding to his diary that Josephine would "hamper" him less than any woman he'd met. When, barely three years after they had married, she was persuaded to leave New York for Greenland in 1891 with her husband, she had no idea that she would eventually sacrifice her life and her happiness for polar exploration.

Born into a wealthy family of Washington intellectuals, Josephine grew up a keen outdoorswoman who could hunt and shoot. Nevertheless, American newspapers were scandalized at the idea of a woman joining an Arctic expedition; Josephine, too, had her own doubts. Love and loyalty, however, overcame any qualms.

The Peary North Greenland Expedition of 1891 did not start auspiciously: While unloading their ship on the wild Greenland coast, the arm of an iron tiller suddenly swung around and broke her husband's leg. For the next three months, Josephine became his nurse and his counselor, caring for his battered limb and his bruised ego. The other members of the team continued with their work, constructing a dwelling and getting prepared for the long polar winter.

Redcliffe House was their home, a small but cozy prefabricated hut. The mess room contained the kitchen, the general living quarters, and bunks for most of the team. The Pearys had a tiny, private bedroom; Josephine lined the walls with red blankets and decorated their bed with the Stars and Stripes.

As her husband hoped, local Inuit soon came, drawn by stories of the outsiders with bushy eyebrows who had landed on their shore. When they first met the Pearys, the Inuit were not quite sure who was the man and who was the woman. In true Inuit fashion, they poked and prodded the Pearys and tried to get a good look around the camp. For the next 12 months, they were Josephine Peary's main preoccupation.

She was as obsessed with cleanliness as the Inuit were indifferent to it. Her whole sojourn in the Arctic was a constant battle against Inuit smells and Inuit parasites. Peary described them as "the queerest, dirtiest looking individuals" that she had ever met; she couldn't understand why they didn't wash, and she couldn't bear their food. Peary allowed them into the bunkhouse to prepare the skin clothing for her husband's expedition, but she was adamant that no Inuit should ever be allowed into her bedroom. At night she and Robert would rub each other down with alcohol in an attempt to keep the fleas at bay.

The odors were less easy to control. Her worst experience came in the spring when, with Robert's leg recovered, the two of them went on a sledding trip. One night they were forced to sleep in an Inuit igloo. For Josephine, it was purgatory: the air was full of dark smoke from seal-oil lamps, most of the Inuit were naked, and the smell of their food and their bodies was almost unbearable to her. Today it is rather comical to imagine this prim Victorian lady beset by what she called "these strange monkey like people," but, by the same token, it is amazing how well she coped. She was only 28, she was still getting to know her husband, and here she was, thousands of miles from home in a remote wilderness, living in a way that she could never have imagined. And she wasn't simply disgusted by the Inuit; she was fascinated, too, and sensitive enough to wonder how the encounter with a party of Americans would affect them.

One day she found herself quizzing an Inuit woman, Klayuh, on the relatively small size of her family when suddenly the woman ran out in tears. The other women explained why: Klayuh had recently had to kill her baby after her husband died, leaving her with three children. She realized that she wouldn't be able to find a new partner to take on so many children, so she reduced the size of her family. Infanticide was a sad but necessary part of Inuit culture at this time.

1908: Agnes Deans Cameron Takes the Mackenzie River to the Arctic Circle

Agnes Deans Cameron was a teacher and an early campaigner for women's rights in Canada. She began her career as a head teacher but was controversially fired after repeated arguments with her local school board. Banned from teaching, she moved to the United States, and took up a new career as a journalist specializing in Canadian issues. In 1908, she packed her camera and her Underwood portable typewriter and headed north from Chicago with her niece, Jessie. Their aim was to go somewhere "un-spoilt by Cook's Tours." They traveled first by train, then by stagecoach, and then, most memorably, in a canoe up the Mackenzie River. The Hudson Bay Company had been trading and organizing travel in the Canadian Arctic, but it was still a very arduous trip that included 90 miles of rapids on the Athabasca River. It was summer, so their main enemy was not the cold but the swarms of mosquitoes that attacked "each one of our four million pores." The main business of Cameron's journey was to meet and write about the Native Americans and Inuit who lived in the Arctic. Though she clearly saw how women were treated as second-class citizens, she was sympathetic to local culture. She described Inuit men as "the most splendid specimens of physical manhood that I have seen" and approved of the independence and freedom of their children. She could even see an argument for polygamy, as a practical solution to the shortage of men. Cameron wrote a very successful book, *The New North*, based on her

WOMEN'S WORK: HOW TO PREPARE A SEALSKIN

Scrape the inside of the skin to get rid of as much fat as possible.
Stretch it tight and leave to dry.
Chew the dried skin to remove any remaining grease.
Dry and scrape again, in order to break the fibers down and further
soften the skins.

Traditionally, Inuit women were expected to chew at least two skins per
session, but they were allowed to rest their jaws on alternate days.

experiences, which once again put her in the public eye. Sadly, just a
few years later, she developed appendicitis and died.

1928: Louise Arner Boyd Joins the Search for Amundsen

Louise Arner Boyd was the first woman to plan and organize a large-
scale Arctic expedition. Born into a very rich family from San Francisco, she began traveling in her early 30s. She made her first visit to
the Arctic in 1926 and went back regularly after that. In 1928, she offered her services and her ship to the international effort to locate the
Norwegian explorer Roald Amundsen, whose plane had disappeared
while searching for another missing explorer, the Italian Umberto
Nobile. The search was fruitless, but it brought Boyd into contact
with leading polar scientists and Arctic experts whom she later

A GOURMET'S GUIDE TO INUIT CUISINE

Unlike Josephine Peary, Agnes Deans Cameron was very eager to try Inuit food and notably unsqueamish. In general, she found the local diet to be very monotonous, but there were some "exceptional" dishes:

REINDEER MAGGOTS
One of the most prized delicacies was a type of maggot, up to an inch long, that lived in between a reindeer's outer skin and its flesh. It tasted like sweet shrimp.

WHALE JAW
The fleshy cushion at the back of a whale's mouth was another special treat. According to Cameron, it looked like a coconut, cut like old cheese, and tasted like a chestnut.

FROZEN FISH
Cameron was surprised to find that frozen fish actually tasted rather good and that, in particular, bad fish was much improved by allowing it to freeze. Similarly, whale skin and whale blubber tasted much better when cold.

employed in a series of expeditions to Greenland. Boyd was a classic amateur who used her wealth to fund her passions; she taught herself botany and advanced cartography and equipped her expeditions lavishly. A very good shot and a hardy traveler, she always powdered her nose before going up on deck and insisted that there was no reason why a woman couldn't "rough it and remain feminine." In the early 1940s, during World War II, she was taken on as an adviser to U.S. military intelligence; after the war, she continued to traveling but spent less time in the Arctic. In 1955, she got her name into the record books when she became the first woman to fly over the North Pole. It was, she wrote, "a moment of happiness that I shall never forget."

1947: Jennie Darlington Overwinters in Antarctica

In 1947, Americans Jennie Darlington and Jackie Ronne became the first women to spend an entire winter in the Antarctic. Jackie had been married to her husband, Finn Ronne, for six years, but for Jennie Darlington, it was, as the title of her book would indicate, *An Antarctic Honeymoon.*

Initially, Jennie was only supposed to accompany her husband, the pilot Harry Darlington, to Panama. He persuaded her to stay on board the expedition ship as far as Valparaiso in Chile, but had no intention of taking her any farther. Harry thought that Antarctica was no place for a woman, especially his bride. However, when Finn Ronne, the expedition leader, announced that he was going to take his wife, Jackie, all the way south, several crew members threatened to resign unless Harry took his spouse along too! They figured that one woman would create a lot of problems, but two women would keep each other company and keep out of *their* way. Reluctantly Harry agreed, and Jenny embarked on her year-long Antarctic honeymoon.

Jennie Darlington arrived in Antarctica with a kit bag full of army surplus clothing, a silk negligee, some lipstick, a jar of lanolin, and a bottle of Chanel No. 5. While Jackie Ronne worked as the expedition's chief journalist, Jennie's role was much more nebulous. She became a laundrywoman, a photographer's assistant, and an occasional cook. With their ship deliberately iced in, there was no prospect of making a swift exit if she changed her mind, so she wisely decided to make the best of it.

Initially, many of the men remained very wary of her, but Jennie found that if she kept a low profile and behaved like just another member of the team, they treated her "like a lady" and warmed to her. Everyone liked her—apart from the expedition's leader and his wife.

The Ronne expedition turned out not to be a happy one. They had taken several small planes with them. Harry Darlington was supposed to be in charge of the aviation side of the expedition but he was much more cautious than Finn Ronne, and the two frequently argued about when it was safe to fly. The women found themselves stuck in the middle as their husbands slugged it out. The disagreements were so profound that for the last few months of the expedition, Jackie and Jennie didn't speak to each other at all, for fear of undermining their spouses.

Jennie Darlington's experience of Antarctica included driving dog teams across the ice, forcing her way through blizzards, and enduring the privations of a full Antarctic winter. Her most interesting encounters, though, were not with the climate or the landscape but with the men who had come to explore the continent.

Although she could be very gushy about her husband, she could also be very clinical in her analysis. Jennie saw Harry as a typical ex-serviceman who wasn't comfortable with the uncertain freedoms of peacetime. He saw this expedition as a way to return to a more ordered existence where he might find himself. Expeditions, Harry quipped to Jennie, had the same challenges as war, without all the dead bodies.

There was little glory, however, in the cramped hut that they shared for a year, and the all-in-it-together spirit quickly dissipated. The men stole each other's food and spent the evenings complaining. At the height of the war between Harry and Commander Ronne, the expedition split into two factions at the communal dinner table, with rival supporters at either end.

Unsurprisingly, many of the men spent a lot of time thinking about women. Some went to Jennie for advice on their girlfriends; some visited the sick bay just to catch glimpses of women's bodies in medical textbooks. A few men became so tense that they refused to watch certain films, because the actresses reminded them of their sweethearts back home.

In spite of all this tension and strife, Jennie rejoiced in the experience and, after six months, she became pregnant—the world's first baby to be conceived in Antarctica. Initially, Jennie didn't want to tell Harry, because he was so caught up in all the arguments with Finn Ronne. When she finally plucked up courage, Harry was overwhelmed with joy. Jennie had lost seven pounds in the first few months of her pregnancy, so at first she was able to hide it from the others, though she did reveal the truth to her closest friends. She did not tell them directly, but they soon got the message when she sat down in front of them and munched her way through a whole jar of pickles.

HOW TO GO TO THE BATHROOM IN THE ANTARCTIC

Skirt or no skirt, it is not easy to perform your normal toilet functions in the Antarctic. A lot of thought and ingenuity is required.

USE THE HALL

When the British traveler Catherine Hartley walked to the South Pole in 1999 and 2000, her mixed team got into a routine of having a toilet break every morning after breakfast. They would dig a hole in the small entrance-way to their tent, and while one person did the final tidying up, their tent-mate would defecate. The ice in the hole would be just that little bit warmer and easier to dig into after they had spent the night nearby.

BE ECONOMICAL WITH THE TRUTH

While on her trek to the pole, also in 1999, Caroline Hamilton was interviewed by BBC Radio. When the reporter asked how hard it was to urinate, Hamilton replied casually that it was easy. Not true. In fact, every pee stop was an ordeal that had to be planned in advance and performed like a military operation. Apart from the small problem of the screaming winds and the freezing air, often several zippers and Velcro fastenings had to be undone. In the true spirit of teamwork, the women became adept at helping each other unzip quickly in order to keep exposure to a minimum.

PUT YOUR FAITH IN SCIENCE

When the travel writer Sara Wheeler went to the Antarctic, she encountered several solutions to the lavatory problem in different scientific bases. Some had propane-fueled toilets, nicknamed "rocket shitters" because they occasionally backfired; others had the equally notorious Incinolets, electric toilets designed for solids only. If any liquid went down, Incinolets were prone to short-circuiting and delivering electric shocks to their users. No wonder constipation was a common problem.

After some particularly anxious final weeks, icebreakers came and cleared a channel to allow the expedition's ship to escape Antarctica early. Jennie returned to America and had her baby She wouldn't have missed the experience for the world, but she wasn't sure that women were suited for Antarctica—on mixed expeditions, anyway. Antarctica itself, she decided, was like a woman: fickle, changeable, and hugely powerful.

1986: Ann Bancroft Reaches the North Pole

Ann Bancroft was a former teacher who joined the U.S. explorer Will Steger in 1986 on the first expedition to the North Pole via dogsled since Peary's disputed attempt in 1909. A difficult expedition that saw two of the four team members turn back injured, it opened up a whole new world for Bancroft, who went on to lead all-women expeditions to Greenland and the South Pole.

1994: Liv Arnesen Reaches the South Pole

In 1994, the British travel writer Sara Wheeler was ensconced in the American scientific base at the South Pole, writing and researching a book on the history of Arctic exploration, when suddenly the Norwegian skier Liv Arnesen appeared. She had just made a 50-day ski crossing, from Hercules Inlet on the Antarctic coast to the South Pole itself. Arnesen first grew interested in polar exploration when her father showed her around the famous Norwegian explorer Fridtjof Nansen's house in Oslo, but it took her 29 years to reach Antarctica. She skied to the South Pole alone and unsupported, hauling a 200-pound sled. Her radio broke down, and all she had for entertainment was a book of Norwegian poetry, but Arnesen was an incredibly strong, single-minded woman. Her only complaint was that when she visited the bathroom at the American base and looked in the mirror for the first time in two months, she saw her grandmother's face reflected back.

THE AMERICAS

In the nineteenth century, North America had a peculiar fascination for European women. Although it was not as exotic as Africa or Asia, it was a place where the landscape and customs could be just as inter-

esting and foreign to well-bred British women. South America was—
and to an extent remains—an even more challenging continent.
British travelers like Lady Florence Dixie, and later Violet Cressy-
Marcks, found in South America vast unexplored wildernesses popu-
lated by eccentric Europeans and mysterious native peoples.
Adventurous North Americans such as Harriet Chalmers Adams and
Annie Smith Peck felt an affinity with their neighbors to the south,
but they, too, were often alienated by its customs. Of course, America
wasn't all cold, and its explorers frequently found themselves hot and
wet, but the most memorable images of American exploration are of
Isabella Bird tramping through the icy Rockies or Violet Cressy-
Marcks crossing the frozen Andes.

1827: Frances Trollope Reviews the Domestic Manners of the Americans

Frances Trollope went to America in 1827 to visit her friend the radical
author Fanny Wright, who had created a utopian community in Ten-
nessee where former slaves were supposed to be able to receive a good
education. Trollope did not stay long: The Nashoba Commune was a
ramshackle set of barns in the middle of a mosquito-infested swamp.
There appeared to be very few students, and Fanny Wright was ill with
malaria. Trollope continued on to Cincinnati, where she spent a lot of
time and money trying to set up a gallery and entertainment arcade,
which she hoped would become a profitable business venture for her
son. It was a total failure, so she abandoned what she called "the Athens

To sit "legs a trollope": *to lean back in your chair with your feet on the table*

Trollopiser: *to sneer at Americans, in French*

The Trollopiad: *A satirical tract, by Nil Admirari (the American writer Frederick Shelton), poking fun at British travelers abroad*

of the West" and set off on a long tour that took her through Washington, D.C., Philadelphia, New York, and then up to Niagara Falls. When she returned to England, she wrote her famous travelogue, *The Domestic Manners of the Americans.* At home it was a huge success, but in America it caused a scandal. "Fanny" Trollope, in her elegant, measured prose, seemed to legitimize what a lot of Americans regarded as snobbery toward their new country. Put simply, it was a frontal attack on American culture. Her targets ranged from the hypocrisy of a so-called bastion of liberty that condoned slavery and the harsh oppression of Native Americans, to the much more basic issues of the table manners of the American male. Like Charles Dickens, who toured the United States 15 years later, Trollope was particularly disgusted by the frequent bouts of spitting by tobacco-chewing men; she also was rather bemused by American women, whose only entertainment seemed to come in religious services. In response, she was demonized by American critics and caricatured in print and wax.

1832: Susanna Moodie Emigrates to Canada

Susanna Moodie, like Fanny Trollope, was a well-bred Englishwoman who sailed to America in the early nineteenth century, looking to make her fortune in the New World. Ultimately, neither realized their dreams, and both wrote books that were very critical of what they found. But whereas Fanny Trollope fled after four years, Moodie never returned to England and was buried in Toronto.

Emigrating was Moodie's husband's idea; he was a former soldier who had heard tales of the wonderful opportunities for settlers in Canada. He had a small fortune, which he planned to invest in a farm. Like many newcomers, however, he had little experience in agriculture and found it very difficult to tame the Canadian wilderness.

Nothing in her background could have prepared Susanna Moodie for the harsh realities of frontier life. With her husband frequently away on business, much of the workload fell on her shoulders. In Britain, she was the genteel youngest daughter of a family of six girls, a published author of poetry and children stories; in Canada, she was a housewife, a mother, a farm laborer, a do-it-all and a do-it-now.

Everything about Canada was new. She swapped an English town house for a log cabin and the company of the literary intelligentsia for a rough crowd of settlers. For any middle-class immigrant, the first shock was the lack of deference in this new society. The lower-class "barbarians" with whom she was forced to rub shoulders seemed to take great pleasure in disrespecting her and her family. The first house they bought turned out to be a cattle shed; when they moved to a new home, they found that someone had left a skunk up their chimney as a moving-in present. The native Canadian "Indians" she met treated her more kindly, but they were pitifully poor, not the noble savages that she had heard about back in Britain.

Life in the Canadian bush was good for neither her complexion nor her literary ambitions. The long hours, the extreme climate, the

SUSANNA MOODIE'S RECIPE FOR DANDELION COFFEE

Collect dandelion roots.
Wash carefully but do not remove the skin.
Cut into small bean-size pieces.
Roast until brown and crisp.
Grind into fine powder.
Add water.

dry metallic air of the stove—all these were enemies of female beauty; at night, she was always so physically exhausted that she could not write. A house fire was the great fear of all settlers, and the Moodie cabin almost burned down several times.

It was a harsh, tough life. When things got so bad that they could not afford coffee, they drank a bitter brew made from roasted dandelion roots. Instead of beef, they ate squirrel and bear. They couldn't afford shoes for their children, and at one stage Susanna had to barter her clothes to pay the wages of farm workers. Of course, many others were suffering much worse privations, but Susanna also faced a fierce struggle with her pride. She later wrote about the ennobling properties of "glorious poverty," but clearly she often felt bitter and abused. Most travel books are ultimately positive; no matter how great the difficulties, the author usually tempts the reader to follow. Susanna Moodie finished her book with a warning about the dangers of what she called "Canada mania." The wilderness, she says, is not place for gentlemen and gentlewomen; for anyone unused to manual labor, it is little better than a prison.

1873: Isabella Bird Tours Colorado

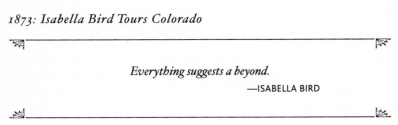

Everything suggests a beyond.
—ISABELLA BIRD

In 1873, at the age of 42, the British traveler Isabella Bird made a six-month tour through Colorado. In one sense it was an afterthought, an excursion on her way back to England after traveling through Australia and Hawaii, but it resulted in one of the most famous travelogues in the history of female exploration, *A Lady's Life in the Rocky Mountains.* Isabella Bird was most definitely a unique woman; the middle-class daughter of an Anglican vicar, she spent much of her early life suffering from a series of strange and inexplicable diseases. Her doctor recommended that she travel for her health, but he had no idea how dramatic an effect his advice would have.

The unhappy invalid was transformed into a fearless horsewoman and mountaineer. In Colorado, she became the first woman to scale Long's Peak, the 14,000-foot "Matterhorn of the Rockies," and she spent much of her time on horseback, cantering on wild journeys through hidden valleys or carefully making her way along dangerous, icy paths. In the early 1870s, Colorado was a wild, untamed region. Its high altitude and clean air made it a magnet for tuberculosis sufferers, but except for Denver there were few big towns. Colorado still had not achieved statehood, and the numerous Native Americans who populated the area were distinctly unwelcoming to strangers.

On the trail, Bird encountered hunters, squatters, cattlemen, outlaws, and local characters such as Comanche Bill and Mountain Jim Nugent, a one-eyed trapper, a drunk, and a poet. He had "desperado written all over his face," she wrote, but was surprisingly cultured and chivalrous. He openly declared his affection for Bird, but, as she wrote, he was someone whom "any woman might love but no sane woman would marry."

Once or twice she stayed in a comfortable bed, but most of her nights were spent on straw mattresses in drafty log cabins, roughing it with Colorado settlers. Bird quickly understood that to get the most out of her travels, she had to learn to get on with people, whether this meant acting as a cook or a seamstress or wrangling cattle with local cowboys. Very occasionally she found herself "Trollopising" her hosts, but Isabella Bird was far less snobbish than many other English travelers, and she had an overwhelmingly positive response to the landscape that she encountered. Her rapturous descriptions of Estes Park in the heart of the Rockies still make exhilarating reading, and there is no doubt of her sincerity when she writes about owning the territory "by right of love, appropriation and appreciation."

1879: Lady Florence Dixie Tours Patagonia

Lady Florence Dixie was an extraordinary, spirited, eccentric British aristocrat, a war correspondent, a campaigner for women's rights, an advocate of women's soccer, and a former hunter turned campaigner against field sports. She was born into the notoriously wild Queensberry family; one of her brothers died on the first ascent of the Matterhorn, another was the plaintiff in the case of "gross indecency" that brought down Oscar Wilde, and still another, her twin, committed suicide. Florence was comparatively normal, but only just. In 1879, she and a mixed party of friends and relatives made an amazing journey across Patagonia at the base of South America in order to, she said, escape civilization and the dubious pleasures of society.

The group left Britain in December 1878 and, after a long voyage via Rio de Janeiro, they arrived in barren wastes of Patagonia. For the next six months, they rode across unexplored landscapes, traveling light and moving quickly. They saw very few other people, and managed to avoid the local cannibals, who were reputed to eat each other when the going got tough but were supposed to be much more partial to white flesh.

They survived earthquakes, storms, and attacks by herds of wild horses who were angry at their territory being invaded, but the main risk in Patagonia was bushfires; Dixie was very careful when setting up their camps to create "contra fuegos," deliberately burning the land in the immediate vicinity to act as a firebreak. Her advice for anyone caught by a fire when out riding was simple: Cover up as much as possible, then ride like hell toward it and jump through.

Although she later became a prominent campaigner against blood sports, in 1878 Dixie was still a keen hunter and a good shot. On this trip, she bagged a puma and a condor, but most of her shooting was for meat. Her party carried very little food and largely lived off the land; when they didn't catch anything, they went hungry. Their diet included ostriches, guanacos (a strange-looking creature related to a camel whose head makes an excellent soup), ducks, geese, ibises, and parrots, but the greatest delicacy they discovered was a tiny bird called a chorlito. Chorlitos normally live off insects, but in Patagonia their main diet seemed to be cranberries, which gave their flesh a very particular flavor. Dixie's rapturous description of one of her companions eating a chorlito is one of the great food eulogies in exploration history:

> The expression on his face, till then one of weary indifference, gave way to a look of intense astonishment, which finally became one of placid delight, as bit by bit the chorlito disappeared down his throat.

Though he did not speak, his silent action spoke volumes of eloquent recommendation, and, as may be imagined, we were soon all engaged with eating chorlito. . . . We had discovered what some Persian king offered half his kingdom for—a new emotion—for so seductively succulent, so exquisitely flavoured, so far beyond anything the gourmet might dream of in the sublimest flight of his imagination, is the flesh of the cranberry fed chorlito, that the sensation it produces on the palate when tasted for the first time may, without hyperbole, be described as rising to the dignity of an emotion.

1904: Harriet Chalmers Adams Makes Her First Visit to South America

According to the *New York Times* of 1911, Harriet Chalmers Adams was America's most famous female explorer. A founding member of the Society of Woman Geographers, she was a regular contributor to *National Geographic* magazine between 1907 and 1935. Adams traveled widely, visiting Asia, Africa, the Pacific, and eastern Europe, and was the first female war correspondent to visit the trenches of World War I. On her early expeditions, she was accompanied by her husband, but later she went alone or with her sister, Anne. Her most famous adventures came at the beginning of her career in South America.

In 1904, she and her husband, Frank Adams, set off on what would become a 40,000-mile, three-year trek around South America. His job as a mining engineer paid for part of the journey; the remainder was made up by Harriet's father. The pair began in Callao, Peru, before moving on to Bolivia, where they crisscrossed the Andes searching for traces of the Incas. The Adamses availed themselves of modern luxuries such as steamboats and the brand-new, high-altitude railway from Mollendo in Peru to Lake Titicaca, but they spent most of their time hacking their way through the jungle, crossing dangerous rivers on improvised bridges, and living in native huts.

At first, Harriet carried ball gowns and smart clothes for special occasions, but gradually she simplified her wardrobe to the bare minimum. The huge range of temperatures she encountered made it difficult to cope. High in the mountains, it got so cold that her eyelids froze together. On one occasion, she found that the only way to stay warm was to sleep cheek by jowl with a herd of lamas.

Adams's exploits made her a hit on the lecture circuit, and she became known as a compelling speaker. She was an odd mixture of a feminist tomboy who argued that women could do anything that men could and railed against their monopoly over exploration, and a petite West Coast beauty who compared the adventure of a new dress to the thrill of exploring a new river. She once wrote that the only reason she became an explorer was because she couldn't have children.

1929: Violet Cressy-Marcks Crosses the Andes

Violet Cressy-Marcks was a very well traveled British explorer who, between 1925 and 1956, circumnavigated the world no fewer than eight times. She was an occasional war correspondent, a sometime spy, and a self-taught but accomplished zoologist. She was also a hell of a woman who treated all setbacks with deadpan humor and kept her cool in the most difficult circumstances.

Cressy-Marcks's expedition to South America in 1929 exemplified her courage and grit. After a few whirlwind weeks of lectures and social engagements in New York and Los Angeles, she headed for Pará, the main port at the head of the Amazon in Brazil.

For the next few months, she painstakingly made her way upriver, hopping from boat to boat, filming and photographing on the way. At first she carried a huge crate full of scientific and camping equipment, but gradually she whittled it down to the bare essentials. Along the route she met a very cosmopolitan mixture of Czechoslovakian, Moroccan, Japanese, and American settlers and fellow travelers as well as local people.

Her river companions could be dangerous and unpredictable: Once she found herself traveling with a Czech who had clearly been driven mad by fever and isolation. He sat in the boat staring at a large machete and talking very little. Nothing happened until suddenly, after throwing away his tobacco and trying to force some cash on Cressy-Marcks, he shot himself in the head. She reported him to the authorities and pressed on.

For her own protection, Cressy-Marcks carried a small arsenal of revolvers, rifles, and shotguns, but the only time she drew a gun was to chase a tiger, and before she could fire it was driven off by a formidable Peruvian woman armed with nothing more than a stick. Her greatest enemies were the swarms of mosquitoes that seemed to be everywhere. Even the specially made, thigh-high boots she wore couldn't protect Cressy-Marcks from them.

When she reached Ocopa in Peru, she swapped the river for the trail, beginning an arduous trek over the Andes to Lima. It was a very demanding journey, made much harder by a snakebite that had become infected. Her party consisted of eight mules, a drunken Peruvian guide, his sickly assistant, and a parrot. As Cressy-Marcks climbed higher and higher, she was alternately drenched by rain and frozen by snow. At one particularly difficult stage, after all her clothes had been burned in a campfire, she almost began to feel sorry for herself, but not for long. She squeezed her roasted shoes back into shape, donned a silk dress, and pressed on to the next stop, where she hoped to find her spare outfit. Though sorely tempted, she turned down offers of coca leaves, the local cure for altitude sickness and most other ills, and sustained herself on the beauty of the landscape, supplemented by the occasional tin of sardines.

When Cressy-Marcks finally reached Lima, no one could quite believe that she had crossed the Andes, but in the years to come, she would become involved in even more dangerous adventures.

AIR AND SEA

The early histories of women's sailing and women's aviation make for a rather interesting comparison.

The first woman to fly across the British Channel was an American, Harriet Quimby; she made her historic flight in 1912, just three years after Louis Blériot. Amelia Earhart flew across the Atlantic twice—first in 1928 as a passenger and then four years later as a solo pilot, just five years after Charles Lindbergh had made the first transatlantic crossing. By the time Jean Batten made her epic flight from England to New Zealand in 1936, women weren't just flying in the slipstream of male pilots, they were in lead. Batten's record of five days from England to Australia lasted for 44 years.

With sailing it is different. Ann Davison became the first woman to sail single-handed across the Atlantic 77 years after Alfred Johnson; Krystyna Chojnowska-Liskiewicz entered the record books as the first woman to sail solo around the world 80 years after Joshua Slocum. In recent years, however, women have been catching up even faster, with sailors such as Ellen MacArthur holding world records for men and women.

THE AIR

1910: Baroness Deroche Is Awarded a Pilot's License

Elise Raymonde Deroche, nicknamed the Baroness, was a French actress and balloonist who was one of the first women to become famous

as an aviator. She was courageous and utterly committed to this marvelous new sport; her love for flying was not at all dented by a bad crash at an air show in Reims, just three months after getting her pilot's license. In spite of breaking both legs and suffering from severe internal injuries, Deroche was soon back in the air, but World War I put an end to her flying. She had barely returned to aviation when, in September 1919, she had a second serious crash—this one fatal.

1912: Harriet Quimby Flies the English Channel

Harriet Quimby was an American journalist and screenwriter who, at the age of 36, became the first woman to fly across the English Channel, just three years after Blériot. Quimby was an unashamed risk taker; this was first time she had flown across water, the first time that she had navigated with a compass, and the first time that she had tried her new plane. It took her 56 minutes to cross 22 miles of open sea. After landing on a French beach, she enjoyed a large mug of tea and some bread and cheese, before the champagne turned up and the real celebrations began.

1928: Amelia Earhart Flies the Atlantic

Amelia Earhart is undoubtedly the most famous of the early female aviators. A childhood tomboy, she fell in love with flying after witnessing a display of stunt flying in Toronto. She took lessons and obtained her own license in 1923 at the age of 25.

Earhart came from a well-off background, but by the mid-1920s, most of the family's money had gone, so she had to support her flying

WARDROBE TIPS FOR THE SUCCESSFUL PILOT

When Amelia Earhart began her career, she took pains to dress casually, in order to give the impression that flying wasn't anything special. Later on, when she became a celebrity, she had her own clothes and luggage brand, AE, but again the emphasis was on functionality rather than flamboyance. Other women were much more particular in their choice of clothing. Jean Batten commissioned a striking white jumpsuit for her transcontinental flights, so that she could make the maximum impact when she touched down. The most extravagant flier, though, was undoubtedly Harriet Quimby. Her outfit for her flight across the British Channel in 1912 was the epitome of style.

> Purple satin bloomers
> Purple shirt with a high collar
> A cowl shaped hat
> Goggles, gauntlets, etc.
> A leather coat

with a variety of jobs. By day she worked as a social worker and a teacher; by night she dreamed of becoming a professional pilot.

Her lucky break came in 1928, when she was invited to take part in a transatlantic flight piloted by Wilmer Schultz. Earhart was really just a passenger, but when they touched down in Europe, she became an instant celebrity, the first woman to fly across the Atlantic. Four years later, she redoubled her fame by making her own solo transatlantic flight, nourished by nothing more than a tin of tomato juice and gallons of adrenaline. Earhart became the face of female aviation, a popular speaker on the lecture circuit and a well-known figure who endorsed everything from cigarettes to women's clothing.

She also campaigned to open up aviation for women. Earhart helped set up the Ninety-Nines, a mutual support organization for female pilots, and was a good friend to her rivals, Amy Johnson and Jackie

Cochran. Her husband, George Putnam, was a successful businessman and explorer who promoted her relentlessly.

In 1937, Earhart embarked on yet another challenge: an epic flight around the world. Her first attempt in March ended in failure, but she refused to give up. In June, she left Miami heading for the history books. After almost a month, she and her copilot, Fred Noonan, had managed to fly 22,000 out of a projected 29,000 miles. On July 2, they took off for Howland Island in the North Pacific, but they never reached their destination. Despite numerous searches and endless speculation, neither body was ever found. The legend of Amelia Earhart is based partly on her achievements, partly on her androgynous beauty, and partly on the simple fact that, like many other twentieth-century legends, she died young.

1930: Amy Johnson Flies from England to Australia

Amy Johnson was Britain's answer to Amelia Earhart. A short, pretty Yorkshire lass, she won the hearts of the British public after becoming the first woman to fly solo to Australia. At least that was how the press liked to portray her. In fact, Johnson was a very strong, driven woman who was both a very good pilot and one of the first women to gain a degree in aeronautical engineering. She also had a turbulent private life and was for several years married to Jim Mollinson, the famous pilot and roué.

Amy Johnson started flying in 1928 and won her pilot's license after less than 16 hours in the air. Barely two years later, she climbed into a DeHavilland Gipsy Moth and embarked on an epic flight to Australia. Prior to this, she had never flown more than 200 miles in a straight line; she hadn't even crossed the English Channel. At first journalists didn't take her seriously, but by day four, when she was pressing hard on the solo speed record, everyone started to take notice.

Meanwhile, the farther she flew, the more unpredictable the airfields became. When she landed in Rangoon, in Burma, her plane crashed into a ditch, and she had to cannibalize some linen shirts to mend a badly damaged wing. Later, after another difficult landing, this time at a rough airstrip in East Indies, she literally had to bandage the wings with Band-Aids.

In spite of all the mishaps, Johnson reached Australia in 19 days; she missed the world record by a day, but she won huge public acclaim. When she returned to England, a million people turned out to greet her at Croydon airport, and the *Daily Express* paid the huge sum of £12,000 to buy her story.

 1930: Mrs. Victor Bruce Flies around the World

Mrs. Victor Bruce, née Mildred Mary Petre, was obsessed by speed. At the age of 15, she became the first woman in Britain to ride a motorbike on an open road. That same year she became the first woman in Britain to be prosecuted for a motoring offense. In the 1920s, she developed

---

THE HIDDEN BENEFITS OF FLYING

Besides bringing you fame and fortune, or at least enabling you to move around quickly, flying has some hidden benefits, as discovered by the pioneer women pilots.

FLYING CAN MAKE YOU TALLER
Jean Batten claimed that she put on an inch in height after learning how to fly because of having to stretch high to swing the propeller.

FLYING CAN MAKE YOU THINNER
The American pilot Jackie Cochran used to find the Bendix transcontinental races so dangerous and stressful that she lost an average of 6 pounds in weight during a race.

FLYING CAN MAKE YOU MORE BEAUTIFUL
The successful female pilots of the 1930s were front-page news and as famous as movie stars. Amy Johnson spent a lot of time and money on improving her teeth as well more general beauty treatments. In 1937, after a long trip to California and Paris, one newspaper described her as "outstandingly glamourised."

---

into one of the country's most successful racing drivers before she moved into speedboat racing and then, in the early 1930s, into flying.

It all happened so easily: First she saw a Blackburn Bluebird, a single-engine biplane, in a shop window in Mayfair. She bought it for £550, took flying lessons, and then, barely two months after gaining her pilot's license, embarked on a solo flight around the world.

It was eventful, to say the least: Mrs. Bruce survived crash landings in Persia, typhoons in Indochina, earthquakes in Japan, and the party trick of a Los Angeles police chief who decided to test her nerve by asking her to stand still while he put a bullet through the end of her cigarette. He missed the first time; the second time he allowed her to use a cigarette holder to move the target a little farther away from her head. Luckily he pulled it off, so there wasn't a third attempt.

Escaping Los Angeles, Mrs. Bruce flew onto New York, where she circled the Empire State Building before taking a close look at the Statue of Liberty. She was told off but, as usual, she got away with it in the end. Next, she packed her plane onto a French ship and sailed across the Atlantic before making a final flight from France to London. By the time she landed, the plane had been decorated by over 2,000 signatures from friends and well-wishers. Mrs. Bruce was a very successful and shrewd businesswoman; after her epic round-the-world flight, she joined a flying circus before setting up a highly lucrative aerial dispatch company.

1934: Jean Batten Flies from England to Australia

Jean Batten was the last of the famous long-distance pilots of the interwar years. Born in New Zealand, she moved to England in 1930 in order to learn how to fly. Her father opposed her leaving, but she ignored him and sold her grand piano to pay for the trip.

Batten was in a hurry to make a name for herself and realized that the way to do it was to make a notable long-distance flight. Beautiful and single-minded, she managed to persuade a succession of men to bankroll her ambition. Her first goal was to beat Amy Johnson's record for her flight to Australia. Batten's first two attempts ended in failure, with crash landings in Rome and Karachi, but in May 1934, she tried again and succeeded, knocking a full four days off Johnson's time.

Batten followed her success with further flights to South America. Then, in 1936, came her most famous achievement: a solo flight from England to her homeland, New Zealand, in just over 11 days. On the return trip from Australia to England, she set a new world record for both men and women.

Jean Batten was brave, cool, and determined. The press never warmed to her, though, in spite of her striking beauty. She was too aloof and too private a person, a friend to no one apart from her Svengali-like mother. By the end of the 1930s, as Batten acknowledged, the era of stunt flying was over. The airplane was no longer the novelty that it once had been, and the carnage at Guernica, the famous battle of the Spanish Civil War in which hundreds were killed by aerial bombing, had given it a new, much more ambiguous image. Unlike Amy Johnson, Jean Batten was not chosen for war service; she eventually disappeared from the limelight and stole away to Jamaica.

JEAN BATTEN'S ROUTE FOR HER FIRST
FLIGHT TO AUSTRALIA, MAY 1934

Today it is possible to get from England to Australia in just two flights, but
Jean Batten's itinerary for her record-breaking flight in 1934 was tortu-
ously complicated and required numerous stops:

London to Marseille
Marseille to Rome
Rome to Brindisi
Brindisi to Athens
Athens to Nicosia
Nicosia to Damascus
Damascus to Baghdad
Baghdad to Basra
Basra to Bushire
Bushire to Jask
Jask to Karachi
Karachi to Jodhpur
Jodhpur to Allahabad
Allahabad to Calcutta
Calcutta to Rangoon
Rangoon to Victoria Point

Victoria Point to Alorstar (Malaya)
Alorstar to Seletar
Seletar to Batavia (modern-day Jakarta)
Batavia to Soerabaya
Soerabaya to Rambang
Rambang to Flores Island
Flores Island to Kupang
Kupang to Darwin

Batten landed in Darwin, Australia, on May 23, 1934, after a series of flights
that took a total of 14 days, 22 hours, and 30 minutes to cover 10,000 miles.

THE SEA

*A lady who can perform upon the guitar, and takes one with her, is sure
of providing delightful amusement for herself and her fellow passengers
during the voyage; and many a calm summer's night, when the yacht is
idly rocking on the moonlit waters, or lying at anchor with the lights of
the neighbouring town sparkling "like a swarm of fireflies tangled in a silver braid," the music invoked by her powers will come as one of the pleas-
antest episodes of a charming voyage.*

—LILLIAS CAMPBELL DAVIES, *HINTS TO LADY TRAVELLERS
AT HOME AND ABROAD*, 1889

Traditionally, the sea was a very much a male domain, and barring the odd pirate queen or captain's wife, few women were involved. Today things are very different; many women enjoy sailing both recreationally and professionally. The success of modern sailors such as Ellen McArthur and Kay Cottee is built on the pioneering efforts of an earlier generation who proved that women could be the equal of men.

1953: Ann Davison Crosses the Atlantic

It is always harder being the first person to do anything. Ann Davison deserves a preeminent place in any history of women's sailing for being the first woman to sail across the Atlantic alone. In the 1930s, Ann had learned to fly, teaming up with another pilot, her future husband Frank Davison. After World War II, they became interested in sailing, and Frank dreamed up an ambitious plan to take a yacht to the West Indies and begin a new life. Sadly, it was not to be: After they set sail from Liverpool in 1949, they were hit by a terrible storm that capsized their boat. Ann survived, but Frank perished.

She was devastated but eventually decided that the best way to achieve some peace was to attempt the same journey on her own. She bought a new boat, took lessons on navigation, and, in May 1952, set off to cross the Atlantic. The first half of the journey, from Britain to the Canary Islands, was long and relatively leisurely.

Getting from Las Palmas in the Canaries to the other side of the Atlantic was much more difficult. Davison hoped to do it in 30 days but took enough rations for 60; the trip ended up taking her 65.

En route she suffered badly from back pain, found that she didn't have much interest in eating, and became more and more depressed as the weather turned against her. She relieved her tension by crying over the stove and screaming into the wind, and kept herself going with Benzedrine and cheap Spanish rum. After finally making landfall at Prince Rupert Bay, in what is now the Dominican Republic, she made a gentle and more sociable trip to Miami and then on to New York, where her ship, *Felicity Anne,* was one of the main exhibits at the annual boat show.

1971: Nicolette Milnes-Walker Becomes the First Woman to Sail Across the Atlantic without Stopping

In June 1971, Nicolette Milnes-Walker left from Dale in South Wales in a 30-foot yacht, aiming to repeat Ann Davison's voyage across the Atlantic, but to do so without stopping. She had motives other than simply getting into the record books. Milnes-Walker was a research psychologist by trade, and she wanted to find out for herself what it was like to make a long-distance solo voyage.

Her crossing was relatively smooth, though like Ann Davison she experienced the most difficult weather at the end, just as she was approaching the American coast. At one point, the weather became so bad that she calculated it would take her less time to turn back and return to England than to maintain her course toward Rhode Island. Of course, like any committed sailor, she carried on and was finally towed into Newport Harbor, on July 26, 1971, 45 days after she had left Britain.

Her psychological journey didn't end with an inner crisis, but she gained plenty of insight along the way.

LESSONS OF A LONG-DISTANCE SAILOR

1. Yachtspeople are risk takers. Milnes-Walker had done very little solo sailing before taking on the Atlantic. Her longest previous solo trip had been eight miles.

2. Crying is a useful mechanism for releasing tension, and one that women are much better at using than men. Milnes-Walker had a little cry after a difficult first few days and then carried on much refreshed.

3. The occasional dab of perfume can help cheer you up; it doesn't matter that you're going to be the only one to enjoy it.

4. As the voyage went on, Milnes-Walker became more impulsive about small things but more thoughtful about bigger things. Having lots of time to think at sea invariably seems to make men and women more introspective.

5. In the end, when she returned to England, Milnes-Walker felt generally more confident and more open to new ideas, but, at the same time, she was sure that she wouldn't want to make another solo voyage. Milnes-Walker wasn't so much worried about the solitude itself; she concluded that having someone else along to share the experience would have made it a lot more fun.

1977: Clare Francis Becomes the First Woman to Skipper a Boat in the Whitbread Round the World Race

By the mid-1970s, there had been several famous solo yachtswomen, but it was still very unusual for a woman to be in charge of a big ship. The British sailor Clare Francis broke the mold, captaining the ADC *Accutrac* in the 1977 Whitbread Round the World Race.

Francis chose the crew very carefully. She included two other women; Bumble, the cook, and Eve Bonham, another experienced sailor. But Francis refused to hire women for sake of it, saying that "Women's Lib" made her blood boil. She believed that personality was more important than gender, and her priority was to find a group of people who would be able to get along together.

Francis divided the sailing crew into two watches, made the navigational decisions herself, and, once the ship was running, didn't interfere too much or get involved in too much crew management.

When she noticed conflict or anyone becoming irritable, her usual response was to move people around between watches, the very suggestion of which often sorted out any problems. When things went wrong, she would convene an immediate postmortem and try to learn from any mistakes. Her only real issues were with one member of the crew, John Tanner, a very experienced sailor whose ideas were very different to hers. Things came to a head in the Southern Ocean when, on one of Tanner's watches, the vital spinnaker sail was badly damaged. Francis asked him to stand down as watch leader, and there was no further argument.

Francis finished fifth out of 15, which she deemed a satisfactory result. Ultimately, however, she did feel that being a woman made things harder because there were certain tasks on a large yacht that she was simply not physically strong enough carry out by herself. This was slightly strange for someone who had crossed the Atlantic solo, but Francis was always someone who wanted to lead by example.

A BRIEF HISTORY OF THE PAPER PANTY

When Clare Francis arrived in America at the end of her second transatlantic voyage, she found herself tearing around deck in a pair of paper underpants given to her by her mother. She had lost so much weight that most of her trousers didn't fit her.

Paper underpants are very useful for any type of travel. Sailors often take them along on sea voyages rather than wasting precious freshwater on washing. Washing fabric in seawater makes it permanently damp and uncomfortable.

Paper underpants were invented in the 1960s, during a period when disposable clothing was briefly fashionable. They were an immediate and obvious hit in hospitals but, by the mid-1970s, paper panties were distinctly unfashionable and hard to get hold of, except from specialist suppliers.

One alternative is to wear nothing at all. Nudity is common among both male and female sailors, but it does have its risks and pitfalls. Nicolette Milnes-Walker spent a lot of time naked on her voyage to America in 1971. She got so used to it that when a ship appeared on the horizon, she instinctively started to wave at it from the deck, forgetting that she had nothing on.

1978: Krystyna Chojnowska-Liskiewicz Makes a Solo Voyage around the World

In February 1976, Krystyna Chojnowska-Liskiewicz set sail from the Canary Islands off the coast of Africa in a 31-foot yacht built by her husband. She returned to the port of Las Palmas 31,166 miles and 401 days later, having set a new world record, narrowly beating the New Zealander Naomi James, who completed her own round-the-world voyage barely two months later.

2005: Ellen MacArthur Breaks the World Record, Circumnavigating the Globe in 71 Days

British sailor Ellen MacArthur is by far the most successful female sailor of modern years. She grew up reading *Swallows and Amazons* and the famous British yachtsman Sir Francis Chichester's tales of his round-the-world voyages. She bought her first boat while in junior high school and her first dinghy a few years later, saving her lunch money to pay for it. She circumnavigated Britain at the age of 19 and was named Yachtsman of the Year at the age of 22, but she only really hit the headlines in 2001 after the *Vendée Globe* round-the-world race.

It was an awesomely grueling event; not only did she have to sail solo, but she was under the constant pressure of being in a race. Her state-of-the-art carbon-fiber yacht, *Kingfisher,* was full of computerized gizmos, but sailing it was still hugely physically demanding. As well as navigating and sailing the boat, MacArthur had to conduct continuous running repairs and be constantly on the lookout for damage.

Everything on board was pared down to the minimum to save weight; her only luxuries were ginger-nut biscuits and vacuum-packed T-shirts. MacArthur carried four miniature bottles of champagne, which she cracked open at key points in her journey, always offering the sea god Neptune a healthy slug.

Compared to Ann Davison 50 years earlier, MacArthur's boat was a veritable communications hub. She kept a video diary for the BBC, posted and received emails via her own website, and was in constant touch over the telephone with her race manager, Mark Turner. Unlike Naomi James or Nicolette Milnes-Walker, MacArthur didn't have to invent activities to keep herself occupied. Instead, she had so much modern technology that she was always on alert, trying to read the weather, dodge icebergs, and keep up with reports of her competitors.

Her worst moment came four days from the end when she was sailing hard and thought that she might have a chance of winning. Suddenly a vital cable that anchored the mast broke. MacArthur had no choice but to slow down—rig too much sail, and she might have been demasted. The sense of competition had sustained her through some of her worst moments, but now her priority was just completing the race. In fact, she came in second, a day behind the winner and two days in front of third place. It was a phenomenal achievement for a woman from landlocked Derbyshire.

WHAT TO WEAR AT SEA

100 pairs paper panties
20 pairs cotton knickers
3 bras
1 bikini
4 shorts
6 pairs of jeans
1 pair leather trousers
2 "polar wear" suits
20 shirts and T-shirts
10 pullovers
2 tracksuits
2 sets of oilskins
1 windcheater suit
28 pairs socks
5 wool hats
1 balaclava
6 pairs shoes
2 pairs sea boots

—NAOMI JAMES'S CLOTHING LIST FOR HER
ROUND-THE-WORLD VOYAGE, 1977

After that, the records just kept on coming: the fastest transatlantic crossing for a woman, then the speed record for sailing solo around the world. In 2009, MacArthur announced that she would be retiring from competitive sailing in order to work on environmental campaigns. However, it is hard to imagine that she will never return.

As you can see from the list on the previous page sailors have never made quite the same fuss about clothing as mountaineers or polar explorers. The most important thing for any yachtswoman is that she should have some decent wet-weather gear and plenty of changes for when she gets soaked.

Things weren't always so casual. In 1889, when Lillian Campbell Davies compiled her quintessential handbook, *Hints for Lady Travellers,* she insisted that some smart sailing dresses were de rigueur. She advised ladies to bring the following:

Yachting shoes
A good big parasol (red preferably)
A bathing costume
A straw hat
A tailored yachting gown

She added that this vital garment should be made of blue serge to enable it to withstand the ravages of the sun and sea. If looked after carefully, she maintained that it could be worn at garden parties during breaks in the journey.

The next chapter moves away from the specifics of different continents and countries to look at the more general issue of how to deal with new people, both traveling companions and locals. But first, as a taste of things to come, a few hints on the best way to deal with cannibals.

ADVICE FOR MEETING AND GREETING CANNIBALS

ACT YOUR AGE
When Ida Pfeiffer, the Viennese housewife who made two famous round-the-world trips in the late nineteenth century, found herself surrounded by 80 knife-wielding cannibals in Sumatra, she coolly turned to their chief and smiled. "Surely you wouldn't eat an old woman like me?" she said via a translator, sending them into gales of laughter. The best way to deal with hostile "savages," she opined, was treat them like children. The cannibals, however, had the last laugh—they didn't eat Pfeiffer, but they stopped her from reaching her goal, Lake Eier-Tau, which was supposedly ruled over by a female sovereign.

BE CAREFUL TO TRANSLATE THE MENU CORRECTLY
When Osa Johnson and her husband, Martin, went to the Solomon Islands to film a cannibal feast, initially they were confused by the local cuisine, which appeared to include a lot of pork. "Long Pig," however, they discovered, was in fact the local term for human flesh. They never got to film anyone eating it, however, because they were chased off the island when they discovered the local head house, a smoked-filled hut that contained dozens of shrunken human heads.

DON'T PANIC
One of Mary Kingsley's most memorable nights in West Africa came when she was staying in a hut owned by a Fan chief; the room was comfortable enough, but there was an awful smell coming from some bags below her. She opened them up only to find that they contained a human hand, three big toes, four eyes, two ears, and parts of various other limbs. Amazingly, she managed to spend the rest of the night in the hut. Later she would write that understanding the power of fetish objects was to key to understanding the African worldview

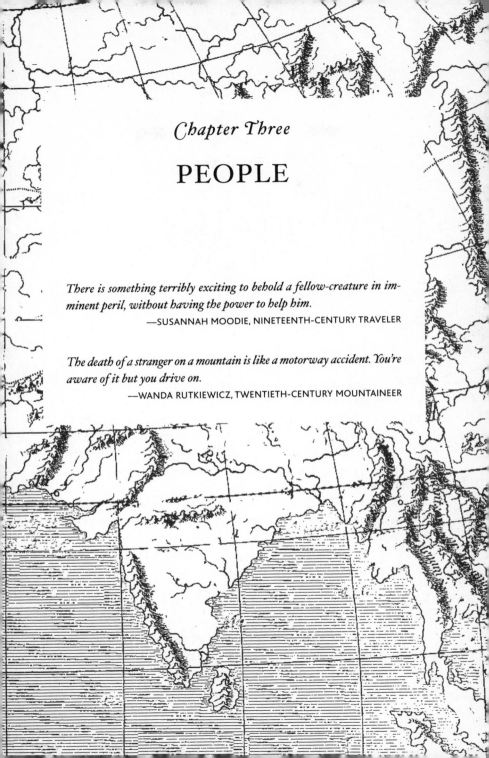

Chapter Three

PEOPLE

There is something terribly exciting to behold a fellow-creature in imminent peril, without having the power to help him.
—SUSANNAH MOODIE, NINETEENTH-CENTURY TRAVELER

The death of a stranger on a mountain is like a motorway accident. You're aware of it but you drive on.
—WANDA RUTKIEWICZ, TWENTIETH-CENTURY MOUNTAINEER

When it comes to environmental hazards such as altitude or cold or dealing with dangerous animals, there is no fundamental difference between the ways in which men and women behave. Charlotte Mansfield once argued rather bizarrely that lions were more partial to native African flesh than to European flesh, but no one has ever added to the absurdity by suggesting that predators have any interest in the gender of their victims.

However, when it comes to interactions with other people, there are significant differences between the experiences and behavior of men and women. Most of the "great" female explorers traveled alone. It is hard to find teams of women or even partnerships, whereas many of the famous male explorers, such as Shackleton and Scott, were renowned for their leadership skills or infamous for their lack of them. So if you are looking for tips on how to deal with solitude, a yachtwoman like Nicolette Milnes-Walker is of more interest than Roald Amundsen. Conversely, it is interesting to look at how women have dealt with the stress of leading big teams, precisely because it happened so seldomly.

This chapter is broken into two parts. The first looks at traveling companions and the second looks at meeting new cultures. For some women, their gender was a distinct advantage because it made them less threatening; others, however, found that they had to disguise themselves as men in order to gain access to particular worlds. How did women explorers deal with conflict, bureaucracy, and simple day-to-day issues such as persuading people to let themselves be photographed? Read on.

TRAVELING COMPANIONS I: MEN

Until very recently, exploration was regarded as a man's game, and most men wanted to keep it that way. Take the fracas around women joining the Royal Geographical Society (RGS): In 1892, the world's preeminent geographical research organization agreed for the first time in its 60-year history to admit female members. Women such as Isabella Bird, May French Sheldon, and Kate Marsden were well known as independent travelers, and as they were all based in Britain, it made sense for the RGS to invite them to join.

Sense was not the issue for the grumpy old men of the RGS. Led by the ancient Arctic explorer Admiral Leopold McClintock, they immediately opposed the admission of women, claiming that females could never be "real explorers." Eventually the anti-woman faction won the day. The 22 current female members were allowed to remain, but no more women were to be admitted.

It was an absurd situation, which gave the press plenty of ammunition to poke fun at the RGS, but it took a full 20 years for the board to reconsider its position and reopen its doors to female members—and their financial subscriptions. In spite of the RGS's change of heart, many men still did not take women seriously as explorers, and even today some prejudice remains. For instance, Arlene Blum, the American mountaineer, had begun, by the early 1970s, to make a name for herself as a serious high-altitude climber, but she found it virtually impossible to get a place on any large expedition.

REASONS FOR SAYING NO TO ARLENE BLUM

She was turned down for a Himalayan expedition because her presence would "upset the tenting arrangements."

She was turned down for an expedition to Afghanistan in case she "destroyed the camaraderie of the heights."

She was turned down for a trip to Denali because women weren't sufficiently "emotionally stable" to cope with high altitude.

She was turned down for a U.S. expedition to the Soviet Pamirs because she was not deemed "ladylike" enough.

She was told by the great British mountaineer Doug Scott that women never make good high-altitude climbers because their eagerness to succeed impairs their judgment.

It is not surprising that Blum soon became famous for organizing all-women expeditions.

Her experience was not unusual, particularly in the rough, tough world of mountaineering and polar exploration. Any woman who does decide to brave these bastions of testosterone and sweat needs a thick skin and a robust sense of humor.

TIPS FOR WOMEN TRAVELING WITH DIFFICULT MEN

RUB THEIR NOSES IT

When the British writer Sara Wheeler went south in 1994 to write a book about Antarctica, she spent many months at scientific research bases. She found that different nationalities behaved differently toward women. Australians and New Zealanders were very relaxed, Italian men were very amorous (even though, as one of their female colleagues joked, the cold weather gave them very small *cazze* [cocks]), and the British were very awkward. She found the bar at the British base festooned with girly pictures and men cracking jokes about periods. In the field, they were even more macho, but one day Wheeler managed to silence them. After someone commented that she had a face "like a bowl of porridge," she announced loudly that she was suffering from severe menstrual cramps. It was one thing to make jokes about periods, but the reality of a menstruating woman left the men open-mouthed and embarrassed.

PLAY THE GAME

In 1975, the British climber Julie Tullis was hired to make a documentary on a French-led expedition to Nanga Parbat. The all-male team and the expedition leader, Pierre Mazeaud, gave her a lot of trouble. He made her sign a contract agreeing to obey to his orders and shoot material whenever he decided. Tullis knew from experience that a sequence showing a goat having its throat slit was bound to end up on the cutting room floor, but nevertheless he insisted. At base camp, the climbers used to joke around and smoke dope. One day, they called Tullis into the mess tent to announce that the Pakistani policeman attached to the expedition wanted to "fuck" her. Others laid bets on whether they could get her to do "women's jobs," such as sewing their clothes. In spite of a lot of provocation, Tullis tried to keep the men happy for the sake of the film, but she refused to become their servant. Instead of getting out her needle and thread, she took to sewing up their shorts with self-adhesive airline stickers.

DON'T EXPECT TO BE TREATED LIKE A LADY
AND YOU MIGHT BE

When Jenny Darlington went to Antarctica with her husband, Harry, in 1947, most of the team members did not want her to come along. Their

main worry, she realized, was that "dames" would expect preferential treatment, so she resolved never to ask for anything. She did not try to be "one
of the boys"; she just quietly got on with her own work. Then gradually she
started to find bowls of hot water in front of her bedroom door in the
morning, and she noticed that she never had to lift any heavy loads. Despite their earlier bellyaching, it made a lot of the crew feel better when
they behaved like gentlemen.

Although men can be very difficult, it is worth remembering that
there have been several notable male/female partnerships in the history of exploration.

The Bakers

In 1859, Samuel Baker, a British aristocrat and widower, was on a hunting trip in Hungary when he witnessed a slave auction in the town of
Widin. One of the lots was a beautiful seventeen-year-old girl, Florence
von Sass. Samuel reached into his pocket, pulled out his wallet, and
started to bid. So began one of the strangest and, in many ways, most
romantic partnerships in the history of exploration. Florence became
Sam's companion, lover, and soul mate. When Samuel went exploring
in Africa, she quickly proved her worth, combining the role of cook,
seamstress, gun bearer, and general helpmate. Together, the Bakers
made two major expeditions: one in search of the source of the Nile
and the other to suppress the slave trade in the Sudan. They married in
1865. Contrary to what often happened in cases like this, Samuel
Baker's family embraced Florence warmly, recognizing her devotion
and his love.

The Smeetons

Beryl and Miles Smeeton were one of those couples that just clicked.
She was dark and beautiful; he was tall, gangly, and charming. Both
were instinctive adventurers. They met in India, where Beryl was a
young and unhappy army wife and he a junior officer. Beryl's first hus-

band encouraged her to learn how to ride horses and chose Miles as her teacher. When Beryl's marriage finally broke down, it was inevitable that the two would get together, but not before Beryl made a remarkable series of journeys through Asia and South America. The two were married in 1938 and the following year made a joint attempt to climb Tirich Mir in the Hindu Kush, accompanied by Tenzing Norgay, a young Sherpa who would later find fame on Everest. During World War II, Miles fought in Africa while Beryl remained in India. When peace came, they bought a farm in Canada and planned for the good life, but they both had itchy feet. Before long the Smeetons swapped their homestead for an oceangoing yacht, the *Tzu Hang*. For the next two decades, they spent most of their time sailing around the world.

The Johnsons

The famous photograph of American explorer Osa Johnson riding on a zebra pretty much sums her up: daring, unconventional, and full of fun. Osa was a young vaudeville singer. Martin Johnson, her Kansas-born husband, was a photographer and movie cameraman. When they got together in 1910, it was never likely that they would settle down to a conventional life. For several years, they toured the United States with a stage show. Martin projected movies while Osa sang Hawaiian songs. Once they had made enough money, they headed to the Solomon Islands for a late honeymoon—with a twist. Forget cocktails on the beach; Martin wanted to film a tribe of cannibals. He warned Osa that it might be dangerous, but she was unfazed. While Martin cranked the camera, Osa sat in the center of the action, occasionally directing the natives but mostly just smiling and keeping everyone happy. Their next stop was Borneo, where they spent a year looking for head-hunters, and then on to Africa, where Martin became an expert wildlife cameraman and Osa his equally professional minder. He shot the film, she shot the animals if they got too close. Every so often they would contemplate a small house with a white picket fence, but they both knew that due to their adventurous streaks, it would never happen.

TRAVELING COMPANIONS II: WOMEN

If men sometimes can make very difficult traveling companions, how do women compare? There have not been many famous team efforts by women; whether this is because women don't naturally bond into teams or because they rarely have money to stage large-scale expeditions is debatable. Those who have been part of a team experienced the pleasures, and pitfalls, of working together toward a common goal.

A Woman's Place Is on Top . . . of Other Women

One of the most famous all-women mountaineering expeditions took place in 1978, when Arlene Blum led an attempt on Annapurna in the Himalayas. She was the driving force behind the expedition, but she was determined to be a democratic leader. Before leaving America, everyone took part in group therapy sessions where they discussed how to work together on the mountain. They left Blum with the rather uncomfortable demand that she should be both decisive *and* give all 12 team members a say in important decisions.

When they reached Annapurna, the group therapy was forgotten as the disagreements began. They argued about who should be in the lead, how much responsibility they should give the male Sherpas, and how much each person should carry. The Sherpas, for their part, argued about pay, gear, and their own status in the group. They etched phallic symbols in the snow, claiming that the yeti had done it. To add to everyone's stress, they also went on strike. In the middle of it all, Blum tried to be a good leader *and* to enjoy the experience. Sometimes she wondered if her training as a scientist made her agonize about decisions unnecessarily because she could see things from many sides.

The crunch point came, as on all big siege-style expeditions, when Blum had to decide which climbers would make the attempt on the summit. This was the true test of team spirit: Would they be happy if only one or two reached the top, or did they all want to get to the summit? A few women, including Blum, ruled themselves out, but plenty wanted to go all the way. Some argued that Sherpas should not be included in the summit teams, in order to give more women a chance. Women, Blum discovered, could be just as egotistical and competitive as men.

In the end, two women and two Sherpas reached the summit in October 1978. Even as Blum celebrated their triumph, a second attempt was under way by two women who hadn't been chosen for the first team. Vera Watson and Alison Chadwick-Onyszkiewicz were very experienced climbers, but their attempt went dreadfully wrong and both women died. A search party spotted their corpses but was unable to retrieve them. The expedition made a muted return to America, triumphant but scarred by the tragedy.

In her expedition memoir, Blum painted a picture of a fractious expedition, but this was by no means unique. There was already a tradition of American warts-and-all "expeditionographies," and the kind of arguments team members had on Annapurna were in some ways typical of what happens when you put a lot of very ambitious climbers together in one team, regardless of their gender.

PARTNERS

The history of exploration is full of famous male partnerships—Shipton and Tilman, Boardman and Tasker, Peary and Henson—but although there are a few examples of women who regularly traveled

together, female adventurers have been notably standoffish. One current partnership that does seem to work is between the Norwegian Liv Arnesen and the American Ann Bancroft.

Partnerships that Work

Liv Arnesen and Ann Bancroft, "Sister Souls"
In 1998, the American polar explorer Ann Bancroft decided to make a second attempt to traverse Antarctica from coast to coast. Her first attempt, five years earlier, had ended at the South Pole.

She contacted Liv Arnesen, the Norwegian skier, who had traveled solo to the South Pole in 1994, and invited her to come to the United States to discuss a joint expedition. Arnesen was not at all sure. She was used to traveling on her own and had strong feelings about the type of person that she *wouldn't* want as a partner: publicity hounds, chatterboxes, and anyone who was more in love with the *idea* of exploration than the reality. Ann Bancroft, fortunately, is none of these things.

Bancroft's research had convinced her that she *needed* Arnesen to come on board; there was simply no one else out there with the same experience. Fortunately, the women hit it off immediately. Both were very strong-willed, driven individuals, and they were very committed to the educational side of the expedition. As Arnesen put it, in Bancroft she found her *søstersjel,* her "sister soul."

The expedition, however, did not run smoothly. Initially, the women found it hard to find sponsorship, and they had problems arranging flights in and out of Antarctica. When they finally got there, they found their ski-sailing equipment cumbersome and difficult to use. The low point came in the middle of Antarctica, when Bancroft ripped a shoulder muscle after a sudden gust of wind snatched at her sail. Her injury became the proverbial "elephant in the tent." Though weakened, she did not want Arnesen to do any extra work; Arnesen wanted to help Bancroft but did not want to appear patronizing. The two didn't really talk about Bancroft's injury, and the tension this created added to the already considerable stress of the journey.

Ultimately, after three months, they succeeded in crossing Antarctica. Despite whatever differences they had felt on the ice, Bancroft and Arnesen got back together for an attempt on the North Pole a few years later. Their partnership works because, for all their cultural and personal differences, at heart they are very similar people who share strong core values. If you are lucky enough to find a "sister soul," hang on to her tight.

Partnerships that Don't Work

Freya Stark and Gertrude Caton-Thompson, "Bloody Bitches"
In 1937, the famous desert explorer Freya Stark teamed up with the famous archaeologist Gertrude Caton-Thompson for what should have been a famous expedition to southern Arabia. Both women were at the top of their game, and both hoped to benefit from each other's company. Stark wanted to watch a professional archaeologist at work, and Caton-Thompson hoped that Stark's travel skills and local knowledge would open many doors.

They returned with impressive results: Caton-Thompson led an exemplary excavation of some fifth-century B.C. ruins, and Stark had discovered the site of Cana, the ancient port. However, this expedition went down in history as a model of an ill-conceived partnership.

Caton-Thompson was essentially a bluestocking and a scientist. She liked things to happen in an orderly fashion; her goal was very clear, and she pursued it relentlessly. Stark, however, was an amateur, in the best sense of the word. She was open-minded in her approach to travel and believed that it was essential to make real connections with local people. While Caton-Thompson was always in a hurry, Stark was leisurely, and while Caton-Thompson wanted to keep the Arabs out, Stark invited them in and sat down to talk with them.

The simple truth was that their partnership was bound to fail because it was essentially a marriage of convenience. Temperamentally, the women were very different. Although they both agreed on the archaeological purpose of their expedition, Caton-Thompson had little interest in the cultural aspects of Stark's research and could speak little Arabic.

As their relationship deteriorated, both women lapsed into illness and irritability. The third member of the party, Elinor Wight Gardner, a colleague of Caton-Thompson's, found herself as the third wheel. It did not take long though for Gardner to lose patience with Stark, and the more isolated Stark felt, the more difficult she became. By the end, the expedition had effectively split in two, with Stark riding off into the desert and Caton-Thompson and Gardner making a fast getaway once their work was done.

When she returned to England, Stark tried to get her retaliation in quickly. The first draft of her expedition book was savagely critical of the other woman; Stark's friends, however, persuaded her that it wouldn't do her own reputation any good to treat a former colleague so harshly.

Caton-Thompson's revenge was served cold. In her memoirs, published almost 40 years later, she portrayed Stark as sickly, willful, and not quite trustworthy. Gertrude took great delight in reporting how, at one stage, a pilot had been called in to collect Freya Stark from her sickbed only to find that she had just made a magical recovery. Having just made an arduous journey, he was none to pleased and openly called her a "bloody bitch."

TRAVELING COMPANIONS III: CHILDREN

Several female explorers retired from travel when they had children; like many other mothers, they put their family before their careers, deeming it impractical to continue traveling with young children in tow. Exploration is inherently dangerous, and few people want to expose their offspring to anything but a minimum amount of risk. A handful of women, however, defied convention.

In the 1950s, British explorer, Beryl Smeeton took her daughter, Clio, on long sea voyages, using correspondence courses to keep up her education. When the American mountaineer Arlene Blum had a child, she stopped climbing big peaks but continued trekking. She took her daughter, Annalise, to the Alps at the age of two. At night they stayed in mountain huts, facing occasional resentment from fellow alpinists who were worried that a screaming child might mean a sleepless night. Most people, however, were charmed.

The award for the most adventurous traveling mother, however, has to go to the Irish writer Dervla Murphy.

Dervla and Rachel Murphy

Dervla Murphy was an established travel writer when she had her only child, Rachel, in 1968. For the next five years, Dervla limited her travels to Europe, but in 1973, she took Rachel to India, as her introduction to serious traveling. Dervla accepted that she had to prioritize her role as a

mother over her previous life as a solo traveler, but their trip to India was by no means a package vacation. They flew to Bombay and then traveled by bus to Coorg, in the far south. Rachel showed herself to be tough, resilient, and adaptable. She was a great ambassador and gained Dervla many new friends.

Few parents would consider allowing their young children the kind of freedom that Dervla bestowed on her daughter. On their first day in Bombay, Dervla let Rachel disappear off to a luncheon party with some Indian friends that she had made that very day. By the end of the trip, Rachel was going for long solitary walks through the wild forests of Coorg to visit friends. At one stage, Rachel came down with fever and later she developed an infected foot, but, in general, Dervla's laissez-faire attitude did not lead to any serious problems.

Like all children, Rachel was very good at asking awkward questions at just the wrong moment, but she also had that quality of openness and innocence that allowed her mother to experience things with a different pair of eyes. Rachel questioned Hinduism, noticed how badly women were treated, and happily pointed out the iniquities of the caste system. Ultimately, the trip brought them closer together, with Dervla writing that by the end, she felt a closer bond with her daughter.

Their next journey was much tougher. They spent over three months in 1974 following the course of the Indus River as it wound its way through the ruggedly beautiful landscape of Baltistan. It was a far more dangerous expedition, but Dervla still gave Rachel an enormous amount of freedom.

The third member of their party, a horse they christened Hallam, was as much a source of joy for Rachel and as it was a headache for her mother. Rachel would trot and canter along pendulous mountain paths with the river roaring below, causing Dervla to break out in a cold sweat.

At one point Dervla experienced what she deemed the "worst moment in her 43 years" when a jeep startled Hallam on an especially narrow path. He reared up on his hind legs with Rachel on his back, just a few feet away from the edge of the Indus gorge. You can imagine all the guilt and horror that flashed in front of Dervla's eyes. Hallam kept his footing and Rachel emerged unscathed, but Dervla was in such a state that, as she conceded to her diary, she found herself scolding her daughter rather than comforting her.

Rachel survived and, in the years that followed, they continued to travel together. Then in the late 1970s, Dervla Murphy changed direction, choosing to write books about the politics of Northern Ireland and about racism in the United Kingdom. During this period, Rachel spent several years at boarding school.

Then, in 1987, after Rachel had done some traveling of her own, they teamed up once again for a trip to Cameroon. Their journey was full of friendly banter and bickering, but there was also a new element to their relationship. Rachel had blossomed into a very attractive girl, and a constant stream of suitors wanted either to marry her or to sleep with her, whichever was more convenient. Much to her initial amusement and subsequent annoyance, Dervla was frequently mistaken for Rachel's father.

Bringing things full circle, in 2005, Dervla traveled to Cuba with Rachel and her three daughters. The trio of "Murphyettes" were very much chips off the old block and were as willing and able to rough it as their mother and grandmother.

Dervla Murphy's career proves that women don't have to stop traveling when they have children. Occasionally her daughter Rachel was a burden, but undoubtedly Rachel added an extra dimension to Dervla's experiences, and together they enjoyed some unique adventures. It is fair to say that Dervla was willing to take risks with Rachel because her whole philosophy of travel revolved around living in the moment and trusting strangers. Very few people are quite this open, but there is no question that Dervla Murphy is a great survivor and Rachel, too, emerged from their expeditions unharmed and worldly wise.

TRAVELING COMPANIONS IV: YOURSELF

Whereas all-women teams and even partnerships are relatively rare, there have been many solo women travelers. This is somewhat surprising since received wisdom says that women are more gregarious and sociable than men and do not seek out solitude as often. This, however, does not seem to be the case. Most of the great women explorers

READING MATTERS

Books are great friends for lonely explorers, but it is important to be careful about what you choose.

DON'T TAKE JUST VOLUME ONE OF A TWO-BOOK SET

When Monica Jackson and two friends from the Scottish Ladies Climbing Club went to the Himalayas in the mid-1950s, they took the first part of *The Brothers Karamazov* but forgot to take the second.

RATION YOUR PURCHASES

When Dervla Murphy went to Ethiopia, she brought several books to keep her "in touch with civilisation." Her stash included a Shakespeare anthology, Henry Fielding's *Tom Jones,* W. E. Carr's *Poetry of the Middle Ages,* and Ladislaus Boros's *Pain and Providence.* As she traveled through Ethiopia, Murphy accumulated more and more books until her "light reading" weighed over 50 pounds. This was nothing compared to the seven tons of books that Henry Morton Stanley reputedly took on one of his expeditions, but then again, Stanley used his servants, not his own knapsack, to carry them.

DON'T BE AFRAID TO TAKE DEPRESSING BOOKS

When the seas were stormy and things were generally going badly, Naomi James found it heartening to read about other sailors who had suffered similar problems; one of her favorites was a book by David Lewis, who had endured a famously hair-raising voyage through the Southern Ocean. On a slightly different (though no less depressing) note, Nicolette Milnes-Walker enjoyed *Cancer Ward* by Aleksandr Solzhenitsyn while she was crossing the Atlantic. She did not find it too upsetting because it dealt with a situation so utterly different from her own.

traveled alone or with local guides, and they all had to learn how to put up with loneliness. Although it is not always comfortable, there are strategies to make it more bearable.

Zoning Out

In 1993, the American polar explorer Pam Flowers took a dog team across the Arctic coast, from Barrow in Alaska to Repulse Bay in Canada. Her journey began at the quaintly named town of Deadhorse. Before the expedition began, she made a series of short training journeys to encourage her dogs to work as a team. As her start date became closer, Flowers gradually stopped talking to local people, "zoning out," in order to prepare for the solitude of the long journey ahead.

Dressing Up

Solitude goes with the territory for solo sailors. All the famous yachtswomen, from Ann Davison to Ellen MacArthur, wrote about the pressures of being alone for long periods. Each seems to have had their own recipe for coping with solitude: Naomi James carved chess pieces, Ann Davison read poetry and made up little games, Claire Francis used her radio to keep in touch with her family and boyfriend. Nicolette Milnes-Walker had perhaps the most theatrical coping strategy: Every so often, she would dress up for cocktails and have a wild night in.

TRAVELING COMPANIONS V: ANIMALS

The old showbiz warning about never working with animals or children does not really apply to exploration: Children are uncommon, but animals are frequent traveling companions. They can be trouble though, so explorers beware.

Pets

Dogs

Dogs are the most common expedition pet. Many women picked up strays on their journeys through Africa, but as Helen Caddick, a British traveler, found, the problem is what to do with them when it is time to go home. She did not want to take her dog, Ugly, back with her, but

ISABEL BURTON'S DAMASCUS MENAGERIE

Isabel Burton, the wife of the great Orientalist Sir Richard Burton, wins the prize for the best collection of animals. When she arrived in Damascus in 1859, she immediately accumulated a veritable menagerie:

A camel
A snow-white donkey (then the height of fashion for social calls)
A snow white Persian cat
Four bull terriers
A St Bernard dog
A Kurdish puppy
A lamb
A young leopard
Three milk goats, chickens, geese, turkeys, guinea fowl and pigeons

Needless to say, her pet leopard was very fond of the other animals: it ate the lamb, harried the goats, and frightened the horses by attempting to mount them.

---

neither could she think of an obvious person to leave him with. He was such a chum, she declared, "that I would have shot him rather than risk him not being cared for." Luckily for Ugly, and for Caddick's conscience, a new owner was eventually found.

Cats

Cats are not as common as dogs on long voyages, because they generally don't have the same gypsy spirit. The beauty of a cat, however, is that it can make do with very little space. Naomi James, the yachtswoman, was given a kitten, Boris, for her attempt to sail around the world in 1977. She was not too keen on Boris, but she persuaded herself that he might serve as a feline radar, meowing if any ships or unusual objects came her way. He was an inquisitive kitten who loved to play with the sails, but his proverbial curiosity was his undoing. One day while out on deck, Boris

OSA JOHNSON'S TIPS FOR WILDER PETS

CHEETAHS DON'T MAKE GOOD PASSENGERS

The Johnsons bought Bong the cheetah from a ranch owner in Kenya. They looked after him at their home in Nairobi until they eventually brought him back to New York, where he was installed in the Central Park Zoo. Initially Osa liked to take Bong out for the occasional walk, but after he made a huge fuss about getting into a taxi one day, she vowed to leave him behind bars.

DON'T LET A GORILLA ANYWHERE NEAR YOUR BEDROOM

Snowball the gorilla was another African purchase, bought from a group of hunters. Like Bong, Snowball was eventually taken back to New York and lodged in the zoo. When one day Osa brought him back to their apartment, she made the mistake of allowing him into her bedroom. He spilled her face powder, ate her lipstick, destroyed her alarm clock, and, to top it all off, went to sleep in her bed. It was his first, and last, visit to Osa's bedroom.

NEVER LET AN OSTRICH GET TOO PLAYFUL

The Johnsons captured Ossie and Oscar, baby ostriches, in the Kaisoot desert in Africa and managed to tame them. They were very friendly and liked to run around camp causing mischief. Osa got a very nasty surprise, however, when one day Ossie and Oscar decided to jump on her as she lay in bed—a fully grown ostrich can weigh up to 200 pounds and even a baby is not that light.

fell overboard. Naomi tried to turn the boat around, but it took too long, and Boris disappeared under the waves. She was upset but didn't succumb to grief. Boris's death prompted her to put up safety lines on either side of the boat, and Naomi comforted herself with the thought that she was not really a cat person anyway.

Exotic Pets
Besides the usual dogs, cats, horses, and donkeys, some women adopted more unusual pets.

Mary Kingsley brought back a monkey from her first trip to West Africa and walked around with it on her shoulder. Freya Stark came back from Yemen with a pet lizard, Himyar. He survived on a diet of nasturtiums and violets and spent most of his time huddled up inside her jacket to keep warm. Stark made a tiny harness to take him for walks and trips to restaurants. Sadly, however, he couldn't cope with the European climate. Himyar caught a chill and died.

Undoubtedly, though, the expert on exotic pets has to be the American explorer and adventurer Osa Johnson. From 1917 to the end of the 1930s, she traveled the world with her husband, Martin, shooting, photographing, and adopting a huge number of exotic animals, several of which she brought back to the United States.

MEETING OTHER PEOPLE

Aloha	My love and good wishes to you. (Hawaii)
As salam ale kum	Peace and blessings upon you. (Arab world)
Namaste	I respect God in you. (Nepal)

Traveling companions can make an enormous difference to the success and enjoyment of an expedition, but most explorers would agree that the really exciting part of foreign travel is meeting new people from new cultures.

One common characteristic of great travelers is the ease with which they bond with local people. Dervla Murphy and Ella Maillart seemed to spend their travels effortlessly making friends, moving from one new acquaintance to another. For the lucky few, sociability is an instinctive skill, but it is also an art that can be developed and perfected.

Each region has its own cultural norms, but certain interactions, such as communicating, trading, taking photographs, and giving presents, seem to follow common patterns.

Communication

Do You Need to Speak the Local Language?

If you can, then the scope of your travels increases massively. Some of the most successful women explorers were notably good linguists. Freya Stark could speak at least eight different languages, and Gertrude Bell was comfortable in English, French, German, Persian, Arabic, and several local dialects.

For anyone traveling in disguise, speaking the local language is even more important. Alexandra David-Néel reached Lhasa when other Western travelers had failed partly because of her mastery of Tibetan. According to British officials, she sounded absolutely authentic.

COMMUNICATION BREAKDOWNS

ARE YOU CALLING ME A *KHAJEH?*
In 1967, Sarah Hobson, a young British artist, traveled through Iran disguised as a boy. Her lack of a beard or mustache aroused a lot of suspicion. An Iranian friend who knew the truth suggested that if she joked about being a *khajeh,* a boy who couldn't grow facial hair, she would be accepted. It worked, but Hobson was still uncomfortable because some people seemed to laugh a little too much. Her friend had not mentioned that *khajeh* also means "eunuch."

ARE YOUR BOOKS REALLY "EXCITING"?
When in 1975 the British traveler Marie Herbert joined a group of Finnish Lapps on the annual reindeer migration, they were very interested in her background. She told them that she had recently spent a couple of years in the Arctic with her husband, Wally, and that she was an author who wrote "exciting" books. They did not understand "exciting," so Herbert reached for a Norwegian-English dictionary and found its translation: *stimulere.* Cue big laughs all around and a running joke for the next couple of weeks: *Stimulere* means "*sexually* exciting."

WHAT IS A "MURPHY"?
When the Irish travel writer Dervla Murphy crossed Ethiopia in the 1970, she found that the very mention of her name often got a laugh. More mysteriously, she sometimes would be asked to give injections! It turned out that *murfee* was the Ethiopian word for "syringe."

But . . . Can You Get by without Knowing How to Speak the Local Language?

It is undoubtedly true that gesture and facial expression can convey an enormous amount, especially when they are combined with a few correct words. Beryl Smeeton was no polyglot, but she was an accomplished traveler. When she traveled through China in the 1930s, she claimed that even though she could speak no Chinese, with every group she encountered, there was always at least one person with whom she could communicate. Similarly, when she rode through South America, she was able to get by remarkably well despite not knowing a word of Spanish.

The Language of Silence

It is useful to know when to speak and what to say, but it is also important to understand the power of silence. When Rosita Forbes trekked through the Middle East in the 1920s, she found the evening camps very awkward because her Bedouin guides were so taciturn. Then one day she realized that she was worrying unnecessarily; as well as awkward silences, you could have comfortable ones. The more confident she became, the less she needed to speak.

May French Sheldon, the nineteenth century American explorer, claimed that all a traveler needed to get around Africa was 250 words of Swahili—any other communication could be done with eye contact. Sheldon understood the power of silence as a way to create the illusion of omniscience; it was an important issue for a single woman, in charge of 150 spear-toting porters. As she wrote: "Better a mysterious silence when one is in doubt, than awkward indecision."

Presents

100 thimbles
Many gross of small china buttons
1000 needles
Thread
Boxes with mirrored tops
Two dozen knives
Two dozen pairs of scissors
Handkerchiefs
Dozens of bead bracelets and necklaces
Leather purses
Tobacco pouches
"And many other things"
—ISABELLA BIRD'S LIST OF PRESENTS TAKEN ON
HER JOURNEY THROUGH KURDISTAN IN 1890

Presents are important for making a good impression, but they are often difficult to get right. A poor choice of gift can cause insult or embarrassment while a good present can have a very positive impact.

RULES FOR GIVING PRESENTS

DO YOUR RESEARCH
When Gertrude Bell traveled through Arabia, she was very careful to discover the correct protocol for giving and receiving presents. Important men, she was told, expected either horses or guns. As horses were rather bulky, Bell took to traveling with a large number of weapons; in order not to be arrested as an arms dealer, she hid her pistols and cartridges in antique vases.

DON'T UNDERESTIMATE YOUR HOST
On her journeys through the deserts of Arabia, Lady Anne Blunt was equally conscientious about presents, but she frequently got it wrong. When she met the notoriously dangerous and prickly Emir of Hail in 1879, her gifts just didn't cut the mustard. The roll of cloth she gave him looked plain next to his silk jerd, and the Winchester repeating rifle, which she thought would amaze him, was already in his armory.

DO MAKE IT PERSONAL
When Ella Maillart traveled through Turkestan in the 1930s, she took a swag bag full of cheap jewelry to give away as presents. In order to make her gifts seem more personal, she made sure that she was always seen to be wearing the items before she gave them away with consummate generosity.

AND FOR YOUR OWN PART . . . DON'T TAKE CHRISTMAS PRESENTS ON SOLO JOURNEYS
When Ann Davison set off to sail across the Atlantic in 1952, she was given a clutch of cards and presents from friends and well-wishers to be opened on Christmas day. However, instead of cheering her up, they only made her feel even more lonely and depressed.

How to Take a Good Photograph

Only a few decades after its invention, the camera had become a regular item on every explorer's equipment list. The pocket-size 35mm Leica, invented in the 1920s, made expedition photography very easy, and very few travelers did not carry a camera by the middle of the century. Although photographic technology has developed relentlessly, it still remains a challenge to persuade people to have their pictures taken.

Tell them that your camera is magical
African explorer May French Sheldon got her best picture, a group shot of some men near to Kilimanjaro, by telling them that a bird was about to fly out of her camera and that the best way to see it was to look straight into the lens.

Offer them money
While traveling through Mongolia, Beatrix Bulstrode noticed a Mongol horseman cheerfully posing for another traveler's camera. When she pointed her camera at him, he held out his hand and demanded a payment. Even in the early 1900s, in the wilds of the Asian steppes, money talked.

Sing to them
The American explorer Osa Johnson popped up frequently in her husband Martin's anthropological films and photographs. Her role was to coax reluctant subjects into appearing in front of his camera. She had many ruses, ranging from smiling sweetly at cannibal chiefs to getting out her ukulele and singing to them.

TRAVELING IN DISGUISE

In the nineteenth century, Sir Richard Burton and Gordon Laing thrilled British readers with their tales of daring expeditions to Mecca and Timbuktu in disguise. Female explorers have proved themselves to be equally good at traveling incognito, if not better. Alexandra David-Néel famously passed herself off as a Tibetan peasant woman in order to reach the forbidden city of Lhasa. Rosita Forbes assumed the alter ego of Khadija the Circassian for her successful expedition to Kufra.

Traveling in disguise is not always an easy trick to pull off. On a subsequent attempt to reach Mecca, Forbes was almost undone by a regulation that all pilgrims had to be inoculated against yellow fever before they embarked on the Haj. This would have meant stripping down in front of an Egyptian nurse and revealing her milky skin and European underwear. Forbes told the matron that she had already been vaccinated and convinced her with a small bribe. On another occasion, she managed to avoid the communal bedrooms of an Arab harem by chewing on a lump of soap. When Forbes literally started foaming at the mouth, her hosts ushered her off to her own private room.

One of the most intriguing journeys in disguise was undertaken by the British traveler Sarah Hobson in 1970.

A Boy's Tale

When Sarah Hobson, a 19-year-old British artist, decided to make a journey through Iran to study Islam and Persian handicrafts, she worried that, as a foreign woman, she would not be allowed to get close enough to encounter either. So she came up with an extraordinary plan to disguise herself as a boy: exit Sarah, enter "John": baggy T-shirts and trousers, cropped hair, sideburns, and suede boots two sizes too big. Hobson wore an elastic girdle to hide her breasts and bought a pipe and some tobacco to complete the outfit. Her first test, using the Gents' toilet in a London high street, was an abject failure. The attendant just laughed uproariously and sent her next door, to the Ladies'.

Hobson was no quitter, though, and a few weeks later "John" crossed border into Iran. Officialdom was always tricky and so were police checkpoints and hotels, but Hobson toughed it out and headed for Tehran, where, almost immediately, a boy approached her, selling sexual favors. Hobson thought that she had been found out until she realized that he thought that she was a *homosexual man,* not a woman. Over the next weeks, several fathers offered her their daughter's hand in marriage. In order to put them off, she had to invent an imaginary fiancée back home in England.

Her feeling that she would have a more interesting and fruitful time if she posed as a boy was proven to be correct was time and again. When she was in the city of Isfahan—one of the most important stops on her trip—she reverted to female clothes and went with a representative from the British Council to meet local craftsmen. They did not take her seriously, refused to discuss prices, and only wanted to show her their most gaudy jewelry.

It wasn't easy to keep up her disguise. Many people were suspicious of her pierced ears, so she had to come up with a story about belonging to a Scottish clan, where all the men wore earrings. When someone noticed her struggling with a heavy object, she concocted a tale of childhood tuberculosis, which had left her permanently weak.

Occasionally her disguise fell apart. One night she stayed at a hotel in Kashan and was forced to hand over her passport, which showed a long-haired British citizen called Sarah, not John. A bubble-gum salesman overheard her discussion with the hotel clerk and tried to repeatedly to seduce her, until she embarrassed him with a quotation from the Koran: "Would you soil your sword with my blood?" He backed off. In general, though, incidents like this were uncommon, and she found most Iranians to be honest and hospitable.

Hobson's basic strategy was to be as open as possible with strangers. Posing as a boy meant that she had to laugh at dirty jokes and listen to men complaining about their wives. Hobson got so good at her disguise that she found herself chatting up a 14-year-old girl in a café and eyeing other women in the street. She wondered if the disguise was taking hold.

Hobson made a lot of friends, but her most important relationship was with a Muslim scholar, Hasan Ali, whom she met on her second trip to the holy city of Qum. He introduced her to several other members of his madrassa and invited her to share his apartment and his food. She stayed with Hasan for several days and developed a deep affection for him. When finally it was time to leave, he gave her two presents: a pair of socks and a petticoat. As she smiled shyly, she asked him how he knew: Her hands were the giveaway, he said, and also the fact that she did not laugh quite boisterously enough.

Once you've mastered the local rules for communicating, and all the other particular social interactions, it's time to get on with the more basic issue of meeting local men and women.

FOREIGN WOMEN

What to Say to a Local Woman
"I like your dress."
Freya Stark was an avid collector of artifacts and exotic clothing. This always stood her in good stead with the women of the harem; clothes, she said, "were a subject of conversation whose universal interest never comes to an end."

What Not to Say to a Local Woman
"I like your daughter."
While visiting China in the mid-1920s, Rosita Forbes complimented a mother on her pretty daughter. "Take her away with you then," replied the woman with shocking candor. In those days, no Chinese mother wanted a girl; girls were burdens to a family, not assets.

For many female explorers, meetings with local people were frequently tinged with the melancholy realization that, in many foreign cultures, women were treated very badly. In Kashmir in 1972, the American mountaineer Arlene Blum was once invited to dinner with a local family; while she and the men ate, the women sat on the sidelines waiting

on their husbands and their guest. Only after the men had eaten did the women get their chance. Several decades earlier, the British explorer Beatrix Bulstrode noted that in rural Mongolia women were often third in the dinner hierarchy, eating only after their husbands and their children. Amongst the Inuit of northern Canada it was even worse: Agnes Deans Cameron, the Canadian traveler, observed in 1908 that huskies were higher up the pecking order than women!

On the other hand, though the lives of foreign women might have appalled them, this was one area where female explorers had a distinct advantage over their male counterparts. In Islamic countries in particular, male explorers rarely got a chance to encounter native women, whereas female explorers such as Freya Stark and Gertrude Bell were able to socialize with both men and women and penetrate that most fascinating institution, the harem.

The Harem

In the nineteenth century, all Europe was fascinated by the harems of the East. Artists like Jean-Auguste-Dominique Ingres painted sumptuous images of decadent rooms where naked women reclined in splendor, awaiting the call of lasciviously absent sultans. This kind of art was essentially a work of the imagination: There was no chance that Ingres actually had visited a harem, never mind the imperial harem at Istanbul. Eunuchs aside, all men, apart from husbands and close relatives, were banned. The very word itself comes from the

HIERARCHY OF THE HAREM

Valide Sultan:	Sultan's mother, the most important woman in the harem
Kadins:	Sultan's wives, usually maximum of four
Sultanas:	Aunts and sisters of sultan
Concubines:	Odalisques chosen to sleep with the sultan
Odalisques:	Servants and women new to the harem

Arab *haram,* meaning "forbidden." European women, however, were allowed to enter both the grand regal harems and the smaller rooms where Persian and Arab women lived in isolation.

The most famous harem was the Grand Seraglio of the Ottoman sultan in Constantinople, which was sometimes home to thousands of women. Contrary to popular myth, its denizens were by no means all concubines. Traditionally, the harem was a place for *all* women, including wives, female relatives, children, and sometimes hundreds of female servants. A few women in the Ottoman harem exerted considerable political power.

The first Westerner to write about the Ottoman harem was Lady Mary Wortley Montagu, the wife of a British ambassador posted to Istanbul in 1716. Contrary to expectations—and to the fictitious accounts of previous male travelers—Wortley Montagu reported that the harem was not a prison but rather a refuge. She maintained that Muslim women were, in fact, less restricted than Western women, living in "uninterrupted pleasure exempt from cares; their whole time being spent in visiting, bathing, or the agreeable amusement of spending money, and inventing new fashions." A husband's job, she said, was to earn money, while a wife's job was to spend it. Furthermore, Wortley Montagu denied that the infamous veil was a restriction. On the contrary, it gave women unparalleled freedom, allowing them to conduct their affairs in private, gliding anonymously through the streets of Constantinople to assignations with their lovers.

The next English visitor to the imperial harem was Lady Elizabeth Craven, who passed through Istanbul in the 1780s. Her reports, published as a series of letters, were less flattering, depicting the harem a temple of idleness, populated by listless, decadent women. She agreed with Montagu, though, that the anonymity of the veil and the exclusion of men from the harem allowed women to conduct secret love affairs. "I never saw a country were women may enjoy so much freedom and liberty," she wrote.

Victorian travelers were generally more censorious. Isabella Bird visited the royal harem in Tehran in 1891 and found women who were bored beyond belief. They were interested in her, she said, because they "never went anywhere or saw anything." Bird was scathing about the insularity of the harem, referring to it as "a pit of petty jealousies and hatreds." Gertrude Bell, a later traveler, was more generous about the royal harem of Arabia, but ultimately she, too, reported that Arab women were treated like dogs.

Later travelers from the 1920s and 1930s, such as Freya Stark and Rosita Forbes, were less judgmental. Forbes based her alter ego, Khadija, on the wife of a local sheikh whom she met in a harem in Arabia. The real Khadija maintained that men and women's lives were "as separate as the blades on a pair of scissors." She was happy for her husband to take other wives because they were good company and because they gave her a welcome respite from the drudgery of continual pregnancy.

Ultimately, a traveler's own values colored her response. Having grown up in a world of courtly intrigue and clandestine affairs, Lady Mary Montagu was fascinated by the harem, whereas Isabella Bird, writing in the era of proto-feminism, saw it as an oppressive institution.

FOREIGN MEN

What to Say to a Local Man

"My husband's an engineer, you know."
Beryl Smeeton had an uncomfortable journey through Russia in the 1930s; local bureaucrats were hostile and ordinary people were reluctant to talk. Smeeton—who had, in fact, just divorced her army-officer husband—found that the best way to impress a Russian was to tell them

that she was married to an engineer; in an era of Stakhanovism and Five Year Plans, it always seemed to do the trick.

Nothing.
When Louisa Jebb and her mysterious companion, "L," journeyed through Turkey in 1907, local dignitaries invariably wanted to meet them. At Nicaea, the local governor turned up on a horse. First they tried speaking in Turkish, then in English, and then in French, but they simply couldn't understand each other. The governor was unembarrassed, though. He simply sat down, looked at their camp, and smiled in silence.

"Hi."
In 1999, Caroline Hamilton and a team of British women put together an expedition to the South Pole. It was very difficult to get sponsorship, and they arrived in South America without having secured the full cost of the expedition. While in Punta Arenas in Chile, waiting for a ship to Antarctica, they got to chatting with a man in a bar. He turned out to be a rich entrepreneur who ran a charity and was happy to hand over $30,000 to the team's coffers. It's good to talk.

What Not to Say to a Local Man
"I'll show you!"
During expedition to Kufra, in the Libyan Sahara, Rosita Forbes was continually frustrated by her guides who seemed to take forever to break camp and move off. So one day, shouting "I'll show you," she stomped off into the desert. This had the desired effect of getting them started but destroyed any rapport that she might have built up. Immediately they began discussing the strange ways of the Christians.

Dealing with Sexual Advances
It is a sad fact that unwanted sexual advances have always been one of the realities that separate female travelers from their male counterparts. This is not to say that men are never threatened—think of T. E. Lawrence's account of being raped in a Turkish jail—but, at least according to most of their published accounts, sexual harassment is an uncommon problem for men.

For women, the situation is very different. Sexual advances range from relatively benign romantic pestering to the harsh reality of rape. When Rosie Swale, a young British traveler, hitched from London to Moscow in the late 1960s, she was propositioned on several occasions. Her worst moment came in Pakistan, where she was raped by three shepherds. It was a very brutal encounter, which she was surprisingly candid about it in her autobiography.

Fortunately, Swale's story is the exception rather than the rule. In most of their accounts, women travelers have been able to get rid of pests using a variety of strategies.

Burp Your Way Out of Trouble

Sarah Hobson was continually pestered by men on her journey around Iran. Disguised as a youth, she was solicited by a young male prostitute in Tehran; revealed as a woman, she was harassed by everyone from policemen to bubble-gum salesmen. When a doctor tried to seduce her, she put him off by repeatedly belching.

Be Prepared

When the ever-pragmatic Ella Maillart visited Turkestan in 1932, she had heard so many rape stories that she packed a tube of Neo-Salvarsan, a treatment for syphilis.

Make Yourself Ugly

When Charlotte Mansfield traveled through Africa in the 1909, she was warned that every man would desire her because she had such beautiful hair. If only she could develop a squint, all would be fine, one old colonial advised her.

Decisive Action and Patience

On two occasions, when Dervla Murphy was traveling with her daughter, Rachel, she found herself locked into rooms with men who wanted to seduce her or, worse, to seduce her daughter. In Baltistan, an army medical officer lured Dervla and Rachel into a hospital, pulled out a family album, told them how lonely he was, and then jumped on Dervla and tried to kiss her. She thwacked him on the head with her stick, and he desisted. Thirteen years later, she found herself in an even more awkward spot in the Cameroon, when she and Rachel were staying with the local "Big Man." First he demanded to sleep with Rachel; then, after Dervla protested, he demanded her instead, threatening her with an automatic rifle. Fortunately, once in Dervla's bed, he snored the night away in a drunken stupor, and mother and daughter were spared. On the following morning, he was considerably more sheepish.

CONFLICT

Freya Stark wrote that one of the advantages of being a woman is that you can pretend to be stupid and no one will notice. Playing dumb and playing weak can be very successful tactics for dealing with conflict, but a successful explorer needs to have a whole repertoire of tricks and stratagems to deal with the everyday hassles of foreign travel.

How to Win Arguments I: Bureaucracy

One of the occupational hazards of exploration is having to deal with bureaucracy. The customs man, the liaison officer, the policeman, the visa clerk—they are the bête noirs of foreign travel, the officials with the clipboards and permits who like to say no. Women have had to be very devious to find ways around them.

Play Up to Their Masculine Egos
Freya Stark was very adept at getting her own way. During her early travels in the Middle East, she was constantly battling to get travel permits. On one of her first trips, in search of the Valley of the Assassins, Stark was confronted by a local policeman who demanded to know why there

was no official signature on her paperwork. "I thought I should wait till I got here," she said, "knowing that *you* are the ultimate authority in this land." Her flattery succeeded, and the policeman let her through. Persia, she noted in her diary, is "not so good for your morals."

Stick Your Tongue Out at Them

When Alexandra David-Néel made her famous journey through Tibet disguised as an old lady, she lived in fear that she would be exposed as a Westerner. She did have several nervous moments when she encountered government officials, but fortunately she knew the correct way to behave: She stuck her tongue out at them—in Tibet, that is a sign of deference.

Get Knitting

When Beryl Smeeton traveled overland from India to Europe in the 1930s, she was constantly beset by bureaucratic problems, particularly in the Soviet Union. When things became particularly tense, she would take out her knitting, both to pass the time profitably and because it seemed to spread calm all around her.

How to Win Arguments II

Male explorers often take great pleasure in telling how they let their fists or pistols do the talking. Think of Edward Whymper thrashing a wicked innkeeper in Ecuador, or Henry Morton Stanley shooting his way through the jungles of Africa. Sometimes women travelers have had to resort to violence, but more often they seem to use subtler strategies. Conflict is inevitable, but bloodshed is optional.

Lose in Order to Win

Early in her career as an anthropologist in the late 1930s, Ursula Graham Bower worked as an itinerant medical officer in the hills above Assam in India. In the middle of one tour, her pharmacist announced that he wanted to go home. They had a fierce argument, but Bower refused to let him go because this would have meant ending the whole mission.

The following morning, while she was still half naked in bed, the pharmacist burst into her hut followed by a dozen local people and began conducting an impromptu dispensary. Bower was hugely embarrassed and very angry, but instead of getting into another shouting match, she took a much subtler course. She took a deep breath and apologized for being rude earlier, in the most obsequious manner possible. The pharmacist was totally thrown off; he had no option but to continue working for her. She had won by seeming to lose.

Win by Provocation
Mary Kingsley, the Africa explorer, was a witty commentator on social interactions and a cunning operator herself. On one occasion, she came to a village ruled over by a notoriously avaricious chief who had a reputation for robbing anyone unlucky enough to pass through his territory. Kingsley took an unusual course: She marched straight up to him and asked through her interpreter if it was true that it was a thief town. The chief was so shocked by her audacity that he personally made sure that none of her property was stolen.

Win with a Little Courtesy
In 1905, the venerable British world tourist Mary Hall was attempting to travel overland from Cape Town, South Africa, to Cairo when she found herself surrounded by a mob of spear-waving Africans. It turned out that, on a previous journey, one of her guards had kidnapped and abused a member of their tribe. Fearing that her man was about to get his come-uppance and that she might also find herself in the spearing line, Hall confronted the native chief in what she called "one of the most thrilling incidents in my life." She managed to diffuse the situation and emerge unscathed simply by talking to him very gently and politely. By the time she left, he had given her a bracelet, offered her a couple of extra guides, and allowed her to take photographs of his village.

How to Win Arguments III: By Force of Arms
If all else fails, then, as Klondike Annie would say, it is time to get your six-guns out. Some female travelers, such as Lady Florence Dixie, were famously good shots and keen hunters; others carried guns for self-protection. In certain situations a gun can save your life, but firearms also can lead you into unexpected scrapes.

The Case for Guns
May French Sheldon armed herself with a pair of Colt revolvers and a Winchester rifle, giving her "31 chances to shoot without having to

WEAPONS OF CHOICE

May French Sheldon	Pair of Colt pistols and a Winchester rifle
Dervla Murphy	.25 pistol
Beatrix Bulstrode	Luger pistol
Stella Court Treatt	Rigby .275
Alexandra David-Néel	Automatic pistol
Osa Johnson	Bland double-barrel shotgun

unload." One day, when her porters were looking particularly mutinous, she unholstered her Colts and downed a vulture with her first
shot. Then she turned the guns on her men and ordered them to keep
moving—or else. No one argued. On another occasion, a Masai warrior flew at her waving his spear, shouting "Wow, wow, wow!" She took
out her pistol, fired into the air, and then ran at him. "Suffice to con-
fess," she wrote, "I now own that spear."

Dervla Murphy was never quite so bellicose, but if she hadn't been
carrying a gun on her first expedition, an overland trek by bicycle from
Europe to India, her career might have come to a premature end.
While cycling through Romania, she was attacked by a pack of wolves
that she was able to fend off with her .25. Today she no longer carries a
gun, but she is never without her penknife.

Similarly, if Osa Johnson hadn't learned how to shoot, her husband,
Martin, would never have survived as a wildlife cameraman. She acted
as his bodyguard and minder, downing any elephants, leopards, buf-
falo, rhinoceroses, or lions that threatened him while filming. By the
end of her nine years in Africa, Johnson was a crack shot.

The Case against Guns

Mary Kingsley used to carry a gun, but she had no illusions as to its
value: "Better to walk around an obstacle, than to become a blood
splatch upon it." According to Kingsley, guns were most useful for the
confidence they give you *before* you fire, but they could not be relied
on to protect you. She added that a gun was no use to someone who
had just waded through a swamp. It was far better, she said, to equip
yourself with a good Bowie knife.

Alexandra David-Néel carried a gun on her journeys through
Tibet, but she believed that "the winged words of Ulysses and the ar-
tifices of Juno" were more useful than any weapon. She also knew that
if her gun was discovered, her cover would be blown and she would be
thrown out of the country.

One danger of carrying a gun is that someone else might use it
against you. The British novelist Charlotte Mansfield bought a pistol
for her trek across Africa in 1909, only to find one day a porter in her
tent playing with it. Eventually, Mansfield managed to retrieve her

weapon. She then nailed a paper target to a tree and shot it to pieces. Her "boys" left her tent well alone after that.

HOW TO MAKE YOURSELF INVULNERABLE TO BULLETS

1. At night, boil a hoopoe bird in a pot at the Talisman Gate in Baghdad. Ignore the devils who will menace and test you.
2. When the breast bone comes to the surface, take it out and tie it to your arm.
3. You are now bullet proof—until you take it off.

—AS RELATED TO FREYA STARK BY HER ARAB TEACHER

SEXPLORATION

It is important that travelers are prepared for occasional conflict and even violence, but such episodes are the exception rather than the rule. Expedition sex and romance are also unusual, at least according to most personal accounts, but, nevertheless, love has always seemed to find a way.

For the male explorers of the late nineteenth and early twentieth centuries, casual sexual encounters were not uncommon. Several polar explorers enjoyed Inuit lovers, and the descendants of their love children still can be found in villages scattered around the Arctic. Female explorers from the same period, tended to be more constant with their affections and were noticeably more likely to marry their exotic lovers.

Some of the most interesting "sexploration" took place in the deserts of the Middle East and North Africa, where the contradictory strains of Islamic chastity and Eastern sensuality somehow managed to coexist.

Lady Jane Digby was known as one of the great beauties of nineteenth-century Europe. When, in March 1854, British newspapers published the shocking news that she had married an Arab sheikh, Medjuel el Mezrab, no one was really that surprised. It was the latest in a long line of scandals that had begun at the age of 17, when she was very publicly divorced from her first husband and the details of her love affairs were splashed over the front page of the *Times* of London. She married three times and counted among her many extramarital lovers the King of Bavaria and an Albanian bandit general. She found her greatest happiness though when she married a flamboyant Arab sheikh 20 years her younger. Medjuel el Mezrab was a quiet but fierce Bedouin warrior. He liked to ride through the desert with a hawk on his wrist and a pistol at his waist. Digby confided to her diary that he was a passionate lover, and their sex life continued well into her 60s. Digby was not a hedonist nor was she prude; she discussed the sex secrets of the harem with female friends and was a one-time confidante of Sir Richard Burton, the famous explorer and writer on Eastern eroticism.

THE FOODS OF LOVE

Green peas, boiled with onions, cinnamon, ginger, and cardamom for
stamina and libido

The macerated fruit of the mastic tree mixed with oil and honey, to be
drunk first thing in the morning to aid arousal

A glass of thick honey, 20 almonds, and 100 pine nuts, to be drunk before
going to bed, three nights in a row

Melted fat from the hump of a camel, to be applied to the male member
just before coition

Ground-down cardamom or cubeb-pepper on the tip of the male
member

Ass's milk, to be applied all over the male member

The urine of a jackal rubbed on the bodies of both the man and woman

—APHRODISIACS SUGGESTED IN *THE PERFUMED GARDEN
OF THE CHEIK NEFZAOUI*, THE CLASSIC ARABIC EROTIC
TEXT, AS TRANSLATED BY SIR RICHARD BURTON.
BURTON'S MAGNUM OPUS, A FOLLOW-UP ENTITLED
THE SCENTED GARDEN, WAS DESTROYED AFTER
HIS DEATH BY HIS WIFE, ISABEL BURTON.

Isabelle Eberhardt also came from an elevated background, but her childhood was much more difficult and complicated than Jane Digby's. She was born in 1877 and grew up in Switzerland, the illegitimate daughter of a defrocked Armenian priest and a German aristocrat who had been married to a Russian general. At the age of 20, Eberhardt traveled to North Africa and converted to Islam. When her mother died, she took on a strange, nomadic existence. She cut her hair and donned "the cloak of the rootless wanderer," as she called it, traveling through North Africa in the guise of a male Tunisian scholar. Somehow she managed to combine deep religious conviction with extreme hedonism. She drank, smoked hashish, and conducted numerous affairs with both Arabs and French colonials. For Eberhardt, the desert meant freedom and the possibility of reinventing herself; it also meant new sensations to discover and enjoy. Everything about North Africa was steeped in sensuality, from the seductive landscape to the physical pleasures of drugs, alcohol, and sex. In her writings, she sometimes tried to tie together sensuality and spiritual development, but both in her life and in her work, as psychologist Sigmund Freud might have put it, the erotic seems often to have been balanced with a Thanatal drive towards self destruction. Neither marriage to an Algerian cavalryman nor syphilis changed her promiscuous behavior; only her strange, unexpected death in a desert flash flood put an end to her wandering.

Outwardly, Margaret Fountaine was much more conventional. She was a Victorian butterfly collector who between 1895–1940 spent most of her life traveling the world, from Europe to Africa to Australia and the Americas, amassing a huge collection. In her diary, however, made public almost 40 years after her death, alongside her lepidopteral peregrinations she recorded the ups and downs of her complicated romantic life. She revealed how she enjoyed the attentions of free-thinking German barons, ardent Italians, and lovelorn British diplomats before ultimately succumbing to the allure of a Syrian dragoman, Khalil Neimy, who covered her in passionate kisses and constantly declared how much he loved her legs. He was 15 years younger than Fountaine and, as she later discovered, already had a wife, but he was as ardent as he was tenacious. Though Fountaine was sometimes repelled by the animal side of his nature, he succeeded where other men had failed, becoming her lifelong companion and lover.

Chapter Four

WOMEN TRAVEL TO VENUS, MEN TRAVEL TO MARS

A Lady an explorer? A traveller in skirts?
The notion's just a trifle too seraphic:
Let them stay and mind the babies, or hem our ragged shirts;
But they mustn't, can't, and shan't be geographic

—*PUNCH*, NINETEENTH-CENTURY BRITISH MAGAZINE

One of the chief difficulties in a woman's undertaking an expedition of
this nature is that every man believes he knows better what should be
done than she.

—ANNIE PECK, TWENTIETH-CENTURY MOUNTAINEER

Margaret Fuller, the nineteenth-century American journalist and feminist, wrote that in real life there are no wholly masculine men or purely feminine women. Gertrude Bell, the British traveler, complicated the argument when she wrote that she sometimes felt that, on expeditions, she was being treated like a third sex. The differences between men and women has been the running theme of the first three chapters of this book; this chapter confronts the subject head on, comparing five pairs of explorers, male and female, who either made exactly the same the journey or had very similar careers.

ELLA MAILLART AND PETER FLEMING: AN ODD COUPLE

Ella Mallart
"Kini"

Age
32

Unmarried

Background
Born 1903 into middle-class
family; father a fur trader,
mother a keen skier and
sportswoman

Local Languages Spoken
Russian

Previous Jobs
Olympic sailor, actress, teacher,
skier, volleyball player, deckhand

Previous Expeditions
A trip through the Ionian
following Ulysses's voyage; an
epic journey through Turkestan
in 1932

Peter Fleming
"The Galloper"

Age
27

Engaged

Background
Born 1907, elder son of
Member of Parliament
and barrister, educated
at Eton and Oxford
older brother of Ian
Fleming, the creator of
James Bond

Local Languages Spoken
Chinese

Previous Jobs
Merchant Banker, drama
critic

Previous Expeditions
A fractious expedition to
South America in search of
the lost British explorer Percy
Fawcett

In 1934, the Swiss explorer Ella Maillart was in Peking, on assignment for a French journal, *Le Petit Parisien*. Three years earlier, she had made an epic journey across the wastes of Soviet Turkestan. Now she was determined to explore the other half of this huge region, Chinese Turkestan, an even more inaccessible territory bordered by the Soviet Union, Tibet, and British India. Almost everyone she met told her that she was wasting her time, it was just too dangerous and too remote . . . everyone, that is, except Peter Fleming.

He was a young journalist, then working in China as a special correspondent for the *Times* of London. Back home in Britain, Peter had a beautiful young fiancée waiting for him, the actress Celia Johnson. Soon they would be married, but first he had an ambition to fulfill: to travel overland from Peking to India via the remote and inaccessible region of Sianking, otherwise known as Chinese Turkestan.

Fleming graciously offered to let Maillart come with him. Maillart insisted that she had had the idea first and politely offered to let him join her party. Initially, neither was eager to take on a partner, but eventually they saw sense. It would save money, and they agreed that a couple would be less suspicious to the Chinese authorities.

They set off in February 1935, traveling first by train and truck and then, for most of the time, by horse. The arduous journey took them across mountains, deserts, and remote plateaus. By mutual agreement they carried minimal supplies and existed mainly on what they could buy and what Fleming could shoot. As he later wrote, on a journey like this, you have to decide at the outset whether to take all possible precautions or none at all: They chose the latter and lived off local food and local water.

Their real adversary, though, was not the physical environment but the Chinese government. It was very reluctant for any foreigners to visit the interior, and especially the troubled region of Turkestan. For years a complex civil war had raged, with various local ethnic groups battling it out against the forces of China, the Soviet Union, and the remnants of the White Russian army. No foreigner had made the overland journey from Peking to India for several years; anyone reckless enough to try had been arrested, turned back, kidnapped, or killed. Early on in their journey, Maillart and Fleming passed a mysterious European, escorted by Chinese guards armed with rifles and executioners' swords. The prisoner uttered one word: "Caput." Later on they learned that he was a Czech traveler who had been arrested for spying and thrown in jail for nine months.

In their accounts, Fleming and Maillart downplayed the dangers, but the trip was a hugely tense affair. At any moment they, too, could have been arrested and imprisoned. Local officials and bureaucrats frequently forced them to wait for days before giving them permission to proceed. The closer they got to their final destination, the higher the stakes became.

Their luck held and, by the end of August, they crossed the border into British India. A few weeks later, they formally ended their expedition with a long-imagined but ultimately dispiriting meal at a smart hotel in Srinigar in Kashmir. They had both achieved something that would bring them international renown and immense personal satisfaction.

However, the experience was for Maillart in many ways very frustrating. Peter Fleming was charming, gentlemanly, complex, and sophisticated, but ultimately he was more of a leader than a partner. At the beginning, they joked about who was in charge, but by the end, it was clear that the expedition—or escapade, as he called it—was carried out more on his terms than hers. When he came to list their various roles, it all seemed surprisingly traditional: He was responsible for the hunting, the heavy work, and virtually all the negotiations with officialdom. She did the cooking, the sewing, and the laundry; she looked after their health and that of their animals.

In a way, it was inevitable that Fleming would come across as the expedition leader: Maillart spoke good Russian, but his Chinese was much better so he did most of the talking. He clearly felt that he was in charge. As Maillart noted, when they were traveling through Turkestan, Fleming learned the regional dialect, Turki, much more quickly than she did because he tended to speak for both of them.

Most frustrating for Maillart was their fundamentally different approach to travel. For Fleming, the pleasure was in the challenge of getting from A to B; Maillart, however, was more interested in the spaces in between. She saw the journey as an opportunity to encounter new cultures and new modes of living, and to use the experience to look inward at her own values and philosophy. Fleming just wasn't particularly interested. When they were held up by bureaucratic delays, he would kill time playing card games while she explored local towns and villages.

During the journey, Maillart didn't want to think about Europe, but Fleming looked forward to getting home and was desperate for news. As they rode through the wilderness of China, they fantasized about a waiter suddenly appearing with plates of chicken and scrambled egg, but whereas Fleming hoped that there would be a copy of the *Times* tucked under his arm, Maillart hated the idea of the outside world intruding into their Asian idyll.

Much as she liked him and enjoyed his company, Maillart felt that Fleming stopped her from really enjoying the journey. He was a little bit of Europe traveling with her, preventing her from immersing herself in local culture. *He* never wrote about feeling compromised, but Maillart's account often hinted at her frustrations: She particularly resented the fact that she rarely made decisions or shouldered responsibilities.

Her greatest frustration was the speed of the whole journey. Fleming's nickname was "the Galloper"; hers could have been "the Dawdler." Fleming felt that they needed to keep moving, to ride their luck when things were going well and to hurry things along when they were going badly. Maillart balked at this. She felt that in their mad rush, they were losing the opportunity to meet people and explore the landscape. On her previous journey through Soviet Turkestan, she had changed route and altered her plans when the fancy took her. But though she argued with Peter Fleming, she essentially stuck to his pace.

And so, in a sense, for Ella Maillart it really was a *Forbidden Journey.* The Chinese did not manage to stop her, but Peter Fleming did prevent her from exploring *her* way.

This might be too harsh a judgment, though. Maillart later referred to their expedition as an "unrivalled experience," and she and Fleming remained firm friends afterward. Fleming recognized that in many ways she was a much more professional traveler than he and even called her "the better man." Maillart was always more cautious with her praise but referred to Fleming as being born under a lucky star. If only occasionally he had put down his whip and trotted rather than galloped. . . .

What They Did Next

Ella Maillart

Maillart continued to work as a correspondent for *Le Petit Parisien*, writing articles about her travels in India and the Middle East. In 1939, she made an extraordinary journey from Geneva to Kabul in a worn out Ford motorcar with a drug-addicted friend for company. She then spent five years in India, much of it at an ashram in Kerala. Her interest in Indian spirituality continued after in the late 1940s but the life of sedentary disciple did not suit her, and she returned to traveling, taking guided tours to the remote parts of Asia. She died in 1997 at age 94.

Peter Fleming

Fleming continued to write for the *Times* and the *Spectator,* though his priority when they got back to England was to marry Celia Johnson. During World War II, he served in Norway and Greece and was in charge for three years of deception operations in Southeast Asia. He left the army as a lieutenant colonel and went on to become the high sheriff of Oxfordshire. He died in 1971, age 64, while grouse shooting in Glencoe.

FREYA STARK AND WILFRED THESIGER:
THE ROMANCE OF THE DESERT

Freya Stark

Born
1893, Paris

Background
The bohemian daughter of two painters, she spent much of her early life in Italy and worked as a nurse during World War I

Hobbies
Clothes

Age on First Major Expedition
38

Marital Status
Briefly married to a homosexual diplomat

Jobs
Nurse, journalist, writer

Wilfred Thesiger

Born
1910, Addis Ababa

Background
The son of a British diplomat, he was born in Ethiopia before being sent back to England at the age of nine to be educated at Eton and Oxford

Hobbies
Big game hunting

Age on First Major Expedition
23

Marital Status
Never married

Jobs
Diplomatic service, SAS, game warden

Freya Stark and Wilfred Thesiger were two of the twentieth century's most iconic explorers. He, with his long chin and square shoulders, looked the part precisely; she, short and slightly dumpy, looked the opposite. Nevertheless, for many people, Freya Stark was the archetypal female traveler. Both made their names exploring the Middle East, but their approaches were fundamentally different.

Stark gained early fame with a picaresque journey into northern Persia in search of the mythical Valley of the Assassins; she followed it up with several longer expeditions to Arabia later in the 1930s. Her expedition in search of the lost city of Shabwa in 1935 was a typical Starkian journey, complete with luxury, austerity, illness, and melodrama.

Stark began the journey with her usual long period of academic research in London and, briefly, in Germany. Her goal, Shabwa, was an ancient city that had been written about by Herodotus and Pliny the Elder. No European had ever been able to reach it, but Stark was confident that her charm and the numerous letters of introduction that she had collected would enable her to become the first European to see the city's walls.

Once her research was done, Stark sailed for Aden in southern Arabia. She spent her first month in relative luxury, courting and being courted by Anton Besse, a European merchant and entrepreneur who was reputed to be one of the richest men in region. Then, pursued by his *billets-doux,* she sailed up the coast to Makalla before heading inland.

Her caravan consisted of four donkeys, two guides, and a soldier, regularly augmented by the occasional paid hostage and other Bedouin travelers. Stark instantly endeared herself to them by drinking their coffee and eating their food, even when it meant lumps of rotten shark. Her guides wore tiny loincloths and painted their bodies with indigo; their only possessions seemed to be huge daggers with elaborately carved handles. Stark offered them her cold cream to use as polish.

As they worked their way inland, she collected pieces of stone covered in strange inscriptions; she talked ancient religion to local elders and discussed dresses and cloth with their wives. Everything seemed to be going very well until at one settlement, Stark contracted measles. She was laid up in bed for seven days and only narrowly avoided the local cure—cauterization with a branding iron.

Once she recovered, Stark was determined to continue, especially when she heard that a German archaeologist had arrived in Arabia and also had Shabwa as his goal. Her bout of measles had weakened her, though, and soon it was compounded by malaria, plus dysentery. Her illnesses culminated with an attack of angina, which Stark thought might signal her end. Fortunately, a local pharmacist was found who was able to give her medicine and get the news back to the coast.

In a local frenzy of publicity, two Royal Air Force planes arrived to evacuate her to the British hospital in Aden. Stark had not reached her goal, but the expedition further enhanced her reputation as a fearless traveler.

Like Freya Stark, Wilfred Thesiger was an instinctive nomad. He was born in Ethiopia, schooled in England, and spent the majority of his life traveling in the Middle East, Africa, and Asia. He was well read and could pick up languages, but he did not have Freya Stark's obsession with history or her linguistic capabilities.

His fascination was in discovering and sharing the primitive life of ancient peoples. No bed was too hard, no meal was too meager. His first expedition took him through the Danakil Desert of Abyssinia, where young warriors proudly wore the testicles of their defeated enemies around their waists. His most famous journey was through the Empty Quarter of Arabia, traveling with Bedouin guides and sharing their meager diet of filthy water and handfuls of dates. For Thesiger, the austerity of the desert was its main attraction. It was a place where you could purify yourself, live an uncluttered life, and bond with others enjoying the same spartan existence.

Stark and Thesiger *were* similar in that they both placed enormous emphasis on getting to know local cultures, but there was a fundamental difference in their overall objectives. Freya Stark valued travel, above all, as a way of bringing history to life. Her greatest expeditions—in search of Alamut, Cana, and in the footsteps of Alexander the Great—all had a historical theme at their core. Wilfred Thesiger was interested in history, but his was a much more immersive approach. He did not want to dig up the past; he wanted to experience it in the company of people whose lives had changed little in centuries.

Stark's and Thesiger's different approaches cannot be read simply in terms of their gender. There were women travelers who sought out the simple life of "uncivilized people," and there were male explorers who thrived on historical journeys. Nevertheless, Thesiger and Stark epitomized their own particular approaches, and arguably Thesiger's style of exploration was, and still is, very male. The modern school of macho TV explorers and survival experts who specialize in suffering in the wilderness and proving themselves to local people are very much his descendants.

Freya Stark was perfectly capable of roughing it, but if a warm bath was offered in a local harem she would take eagerly. She accepted that exploration was rarely comfortable, but she did not seek out discomfort in the way that Thesiger and so many male explorers seem to. She was a great traveler because she managed to be both goal oriented, traditionally regarded as a male trait, and flexible, traditionally regarded as a more feminine trait. During World War II, while Thesiger worked for the Long Range Desert Group, carrying out dangerous missions behind enemy lines, Stark was employed by the British government to spend her time in the salons of Cairo, trying to talk Egyptians into the supporting the British. He was the strong silent type; she was a great communicator for whom travel was a both a challenge and a liberation.

What They Did Next

Freya Stark
Stark made several expeditions to the Middle East before World War II, when she settled in Cairo. She returned to Italy in 1946 before resuming her career as a preeminent travel writer and woman of letters. She traveled widely in Turkey and wrote several guidebooks. Stark continued to work well into her 80s, trekking through Nepal on a donkey and voyaging down the Euphrates on a raft for a BBC documentary. She died in 1993 at the age of 100.

Wilfred Thesiger
Like Freya Stark, Thesiger eventually won great acclaim as a travel writer, though he did not share her pretensions to literary glory. After World War II, he continued to explore the Middle East and Asia before settling in Kenya, where he became an honorary game warden. He died in 2003 at the age of 93.

EDMUND HILLARY AND JUNKO TABEI:
HIGH ACHIEVERS

1921:   A British team makes the first ever expedition to Everest.

1953:   Hillary and Tenzing reach the summit of Everest.

1970:   Setsuko Watanabe becomes the first woman to take part in an Everest expedition.

1975:   Junko Tabei becomes the first woman to climb Everest.

1979:   Hannelore Schmatz becomes the fourth woman to climb Everest and the first woman to die on the mountain, falling on the descent.

1995:   Alison Hargreaves becomes first woman to climb Everest solo and without oxygen.

2002:   Tame Watanabe, age 63, becomes the oldest woman to climb Everest.

2003:   Sherpa Ming Kipa, age 15, becomes the youngest girl to climb Everest.

Junko Tabei

Born
1939

Background
Had a conventional childhood, climbing for the first time on a school trip age 10. In her early 20s, climbing became an obsession.

Age on Everest
36

Height
4 foot 9 inches

Marital Status on Everest
Married with one child, age two and a half

Previous Job
Housewife

Previous Expeditions
From her early 20s, climbed extensively in Japan; her only other major Himalayan expedition was to Annapurna III in 1970

Edmund Hillary

Born
1919

Background
Son of a journalist and farmer, he had a difficult early life. He became interested in climbing in his teens and reached his first major summit in 1939, age 20.

Age on Everest
33

Height
6 foot 2 inches

Marital Status on Everest
Married girlfriend Louise shortly after returning from Everest

Previous Job
Beekeeper

Previous Expeditions
Several expeditions to New Zealand's South Island; in an Everest reconnaissance expedition in 1951 and a training expedition to Cho Oyu in 1952

On May 16, 1975, the Japanese climber Junko Tabei hacked her way into the history books to become the first woman to reach the summit of Everest, 22 years after Hillary and Tenzing. As the thirty-ninth person to climb the world's highest mountain, she did not have quite the same news value as Sir Edmund, but, in Japan at least, Tabei was fêted as a national heroine.

Physically, Hillary and Tabei were very different. He was over six feet tall, she was diminutive even for a Japanese woman. In many other ways, however, they had a lot in common. In their youth, neither had been a notable athlete but both had found themselves in the mountains, discovering a natural gift for climbing. Temperamentally, they were modest yet fiercely determined. Both were family oriented, and after they had found fame, both became involved in environmental campaigning. The biggest differences between them lay not in their personal qualities but in the context of their achievement.

When Edmund Hillary was invited to join the British Everest team in 1952, there was no question of including a woman. At the time, there were no British female climbers with any significant Himalayan experience, and even if there were, it is very unlikely that they would have been invited. Some male climbers insisted that women couldn't cope with high altitude; others argued that women would disrupt the harmony of a predominately male expedition. Most men simply did not consider women climbers to be their equal.

By the time Tabei made her attempt, 22 years later, things were beginning to change, and Japan was leading the way. Junko Tabei was one of one of her country's most successful mountaineers. She had climbed extensively in her homeland and made one major trip to the Himalayas in 1970 as part of a Japanese all-woman expedition to Annapurna III. It was a difficult, fractious trip; several women fell ill, and there was a lot of squabbling over who would be on the summit team. Tabei was chosen, and on May 19, 1970, she and Hiroko Hirakawa reached the top, supported by two Sherpas.

Success on Annapurna confirmed her status in the climbing world and fueled her ambition. Her husband, Mansunobu, was supportive of an attempt on Everest; his only caveat was that she should bear him a child before she left. Two years later, and three and a half months pregnant, Junko put in her application to the Nepalese government.

The Annapurna expedition had been financed by the women's own savings (and debts), but Everest was just too expensive. Tabei and her coleader budgeted for £86,000, less than half the cost of an all-male Japanese expedition to Everest in 1974, but they had problems raising sponsorship. Big business wasn't interested in supporting women climbers, and the team went ahead only when a newspaper and TV channel stepped in at the eleventh hour. Cynics said that they only wanted the rights to a forthcoming disaster story. Edmund Hillary hadn't really been involved in any of the organization or fund-raising activity for the British 1953 expedition, but Tabei had to put in long hours and almost three years of hard work before she set off for Nepal.

Although this was supposedly an all-woman expedition, the Japanese women hired 23 (male) Sherpas to assist them at high altitude. In Hillary's day, few Sherpas had any technical skills and all the route-finding was done by the British, but by 1975, the Japanese women were confident enough to allow their Sherpas to do some of the lead climbing.

The women had the advantage of following a known route up Everest, but they still found it very difficult. In 1953, John Hunt, the leader of the British team, had been careful to hold back Tenzing and Hillary until the later stages of the climb, but Tabei was in the lead from the beginning. And whereas Hillary had a relatively uneventful ascent, Tabei was almost killed before she made her summit bid.

Her moment of crisis came a several weeks into the expedition, when she was resting at a low camp. Suddenly, there was a deafening roar as a huge avalanche hit, drowning her tent in snow. Tabei lost consciousness; her young daughter flashed before her eyes. She thought that her time had come but then, suddenly, she woke up, lying on the snow. The Sherpas had rescued her by dragging her feet-first out of the snowdrift.

For the next three days, Tabei lay huddled in her sleeping bag, virtually unable to move. Much equipment had been lost, and it looked as if the expedition might have to be abandoned. Amazingly, though, with doggedness and incredible strength of will, Tabei recovered and started climbing. She was so impressive that she was once again chosen for the summit team.

The final stage of the climb was hugely difficult. The route to the top was covered in deep snow, and Tabei and her Sherpa partner, Ang Tshering, found the going very difficult. The "Hillary step"—a rock chimney first climbed by its namesake in 1953—was a particularly difficult hurdle, and Ang Tshering had to lead all the way to the summit, occasionally pulling Tabei along by the hand. When they finally reached the top, she was too worried and exhausted to spend any time enjoying the moment, and she later admitted that she found the descent terrifying. None of the other Japanese women followed her to the summit.

In purely mountaineering terms, Hillary's was the greater achievement. He led the final stages of the climb and was going into the unknown rather than following an established route. Without belittling Tenzing's role in the British expedition, it is obvious that Ang Tshering was more instrumental in getting Tabei to the top than Tenzing had been with Hillary. Conversely, Tabei had had a far more exhausting buildup to her expedition with all her organizational duties and had set off for the summit scarcely two weeks after surviving an avalanche that had left her hips battered and her body covered in bruises.

After the expedition, Tabei was a reluctant heroine; she did not like all the publicity and razzmatazz, and teased interviewers by saying that she did not know what all the fuss was about: Everest was "just another mountain." Hillary was similarly bored by all the attention, and his remark to George Lowe, the other New Zealand climber, a day after reaching the summit, was characteristic of his own down-to-earth approach: "We knocked the bastard off."

Climbing Everest, of course, had a huge symbolic importance in both instances; Hillary and Tenzing showed that it could be done, and Tabei proved that anyone who said that women had no place on high mountains was wrong. Ultimately, for all their outward differences, Hillary and Tabei were much more similar than Maillart and Fleming or Thesiger and Stark. They were both tough, ambitious, and modest. They climbed for the love of climbing and were willing to take huge risks to reach their goal. Perhaps mountain climbing is just a more singular activity than other types of exploration; the defining characteristic of Hillary and Tabei was their love of mountaineering, not their gender.

What They Did Next

Junko Tabei
After Everest, Tabei remained a fervent mountaineer. In 1992, she became the first woman to have climbed the Seven Summits, the highest peaks on each continent. Like many mountaineers, she became interested in environmental issues, eventually becoming president of the Japanese Himalayan Adventure Trust, an organization devoted to cleaning up the world's high mountains. She continued to climb into her sixties.

Edmund Hillary
Hillary wanted to continue to climb after Everest but began to suffer from severe altitude sickness after an accident on Makalu in Nepal in 1954, which effectively ruled out further serious mountaineering. His taste for adventure was undiminished, and he led the New Zealand team that took part in the British Commonwealth trans-Antarctic expedition in 1958. He subsequently devoted much of his time, energy, and sweat to raising money for a foundation that built schools and hospitals in Nepal. Tragically, in 1975, he lost his wife and daughter in an air crash near Kathmandu. In his mid fifties, Hillary became interested in New Zealand politics and later served as the New Zealand High Commissioner to India and Nepal. He died in 2008, age 88.

WALLY AND MARIE HERBERT:
A POLAR FAMILY

Marie Herbert

Born
1941, Dublin

Background
Cosmopolitan childhood: born
into an army family; grew up in
Sri Lanka and wasgrew up in
Egypt and educated in
South India and South
Africa

**Age on First Major
Expedition**
30

Marital Status
Married Wally Herbert in 1969

Previous Jobs
Teaching English and drama;
public relations

Expedition History
Greenland was her first
expedition

Wally Herbert

Born
1934, England

Background
Born into an army family; grew
up in Egypt and South Africa

Age on First Major Expedition
At 21 he began working in the
Antarctic for the Falkland
Islands Dependencies Survey

Marital Status
Married Marie McGaughey in
1969

Previous Jobs
Surveyor, explorer

Expedition History
Had traveled in the Arctic and
the Antarctic. He became
famous in 1969 for leading the
British trans-Arctic expedition,
which made an epic crossing
from Alaska to Spitsbergen

In 1969, a young actress working in public relations married Wally Herbert, Britain's most famous polar explorer. Marie Herbert expected to live the traditional life of an explorer's wife, spending solitary months waiting for her husband to return from his travels, but things turned out very differently. In 1971, Wally invited Marie to accompany him to Greenland and she said yes, with some trepidation. A few months later, she found herself traveling north with a 10-month old daughter, heading for a remote island in the Arctic.

Over the next 16 months, while Wally tried to make a documentary about the Thule Inuit of Greenland, Marie was an Arctic housewife, sharing her life with the women of a small island community. Her experiences were a fascinating contrast to those of her husband and the usual fare of the polar explorer.

Marie's had been a nomadic childhood. She was born in Ireland and grew up in Sri Lanka before moving to London to train as an actress. Nothing though could have prepared her for the profound culture shock of her new way of life. The freezing temperatures, the long darkness of the polar night, the isolation, and claustrophobia of such a small village—all would be hugely stressful for any outsider, and they took their toll on her.

For Wally, however, it was business as usual. Over the last 15 years he had taken part in several long expeditions to the Antarctic and the Arctic. He saw himself in the grand tradition of the European travelers. His heroes were men like Shackleton and Amundsen, and in many ways he *was* the last "Great White Explorer."

Wally was attracted to the Thule Inuit because of their unique skills as travelers and hunters. They were virtually the last tribe of Inuit who maintained the traditional lifestyle, subsisting principally on seal meat. For all his admiration, Wally realized that this was a dying culture that really had no place in the modern world. His goal was to preserve their lifestyle on film.

While he worked on his documentary, Marie got on with everyday life, looking after her husband and their daughter, Kari. Marie accompanied Wally on a couple of trips but spent most of her time in the village. Initially there was a real barrier between Marie and the Inuit women, but it broke down over time. Inuit life was very strictly delineated according to gender. The men hunted and the women stayed at home cooking, looking after children, and preparing and repairing their husband's animal-skin clothing. It was a role that could be very tedious. When the men were away, the women had very little to talk about. Initially they spent their time visiting each other and gossiping, but for Marie, life became monotonous very quickly.

Marie became close to a few women in particular, and some of her most fascinating insights were regarding their ideas about friendship. She discovered that many women in that culture did not have any friends. In spite of the common hardships they faced, in spite of the shared tedium of their lives, and in spite of the physical proximity of their houses, many of the women had only one friend or none at all.

When Marie talked to them about her best friend at home, the actress Pauline Collins, they listened with envy. The idea of having someone apart from a husband to share their lives with, someone with whom they could be intimate and emotional, someone they disagree with but who would always be there for them—this was alien to them. To her amazement, Inuit women did not even seem to baby-sit for each other.

Wally did not really share Marie's fascination with the intimate details of Inuit life. His book, *The Eskimos* (as the Inuit were sometimes formerly known), published two years after their trip to Greenland, was an attempt to understand Inuit history and culture. It is at turns erudite, poetic, and passionate, but it is also strangely detached. There's no introduction, and Wally barely mentions his personal contact with the Inuit.

Marie's account, by contrast, *The Snow People,* was much more personal and occasionally searingly honest. In one incident she described an argument that she had with Maria, the wife of Avatak, a hunter who traveled with Wally. Maria and Avatak lived near to the Herberts, and over the course of many months they became good friends. Maria used to look after their daughter, Kari, when Wally and Marie went traveling.

One day, many months after they had moved into the settlement, Maria turned on Marie, telling her that the whole community had been shocked by the Herberts' lack of gratitude for their Christmas presents. This might seem trivial, but in a village where most presents were handmade, it was taken as a huge insult. Marie and Wally had not felt ungrateful; in fact, they had been overwhelmed by the warmth of their reception, but they hadn't let it show. Perhaps it was just old-fashioned British reserve. When Marie realized how deeply everyone had been hurt, she cried her eyes out.

This very personal, very emotional interaction with another culture is what makes Marie Herbert's experience of the Arctic so fascinating and so different from the usual Arctic tales. When she arrived, she was excited but afraid. Would she be able to stand the isolation? What would happen if the weather got so bad that the whole village got cut off in the winter? How would her baby daughter react? When she left, she had conquered some of her fears about the Arctic, but her most profound experiences had nothing to do with the landscape or the climate but with the people with whom she had spent time. Her journey took her across vast oceans of sea and ice, but she made her most important discoveries sitting in small, smoky rooms chatting about everyday life.

What They Did Next

Marie Herbert

In the years that followed, Marie returned to Greenland several times. She traveled widely and wrote another exploration book, *The Reindeer People,* about her experiences accompanying a group of nomadic Sami on their annual migration. Recently she has become increasingly interested in spirituality and healing. Today she regularly leads personal development workshops and wilderness quests.

Wally Herbert

Wally continued to explore Greenland and the Arctic. He made further documentaries and carried on writing about exploration and Inuit culture. In his later years, he became a noted painter, specializing in Arctic scenes. He died in 2007.

NAOMI JAMES AND ROBIN KNOX-JOHNSTON: ROUND THE WORLD IN HUNDREDS OF DAYS

Naomi James

Born
1949

Background
Grew up on a farm in New
Zealand before traveling to
Europe

Marital Status
Recently married to the sailor
Rob James

Previous Jobs
Hairdresser

Previous Expeditions
None

Robin Knox-Johnston

Born
1939

Background
Grew up in London and joined
the Merchant Navy in 1957

Marital Status
Separated from his
wife before his round-
the-world voyage

Previous Jobs
Master mariner

**Previous
Expeditions**
In 1965 sailed his yacht
Suhaili from Bombay to
England

On June 8, 1978, Naomi James sailed into Dartmouth harbor, having just completed an epic 272-day voyage around the world. Although she did not realize it at the time, she had been narrowly beaten to the punch by the Polish sailor Krystyna Chojnowska-Liskiewicz, who just two months earlier had claimed the women's record for the first solo circumnavigation. Nevertheless, James's achievement was enormous, and she was over 129 days faster than Chojnowska-Liskiewicz. Most amazingly of all, she did this barely two years after first setting foot in a boat. Yachting, once a very male preserve, now had two women who had single-handedly sailed around the globe.

A couple of hours farther west along the British coast lies the larger port of Falmouth. A decade earlier, it had hosted another record-breaking voyage by the British sailor Robin Knox-Johnston. In April 1969, he had become the first man to sail around the world nonstop, beating several larger yachts and winning the *Sunday Times*

Golden Globe Race. It is fascinating to compare Naomi James and Robin Knox-Johnston: a woman who was new to sailing but gifted with a tremendous self-belief and an experienced sailor, cut very much in the heroic mold of the British sailor. Both of them took on the same huge challenge and won, but the tales they lived to tell were very different.

Naomi James grew up on a sheep farm in New Zealand; she was shy, isolated, and not at all academic. She left school early to work as an apprentice hairdresser, but she couldn't bear the endless gossip of the salon and decided to head for Europe for a couple of years of odd jobs and traveling. Purely by chance, she met her future husband, the yachtsman Rob James, on the dockside of Saint-Malo in France. Their rapport was immediate. Within a few weeks, she was part of his crew; two years later, they were married.

One day James read an article about a French girl who wanted to sail around the world. In spite of being so new to yachting, James decided that she, too, would achieve this feat. It seemed like a crazy notion at first, but when she mentioned it to her husband, he was surprisingly enthusiastic. The die was cast: According to Naomi James's personal code, whenever she broached an idea in public, she had to carry it through.

Considering her lack of experience, she found it remarkably easy to organize the expedition. There were the usual problems with raising money, but nothing was insurmountable. Chay Blyth, a friend of Rob's, agreed to lend her one of his boats, and the *Daily Express* came on board as her main sponsor. And so, in September 1977, she nervously cast off with a large yacht, chock full to the rafters.

Robin Knox-Johnston, by contrast, had a much more conventional seafaring background. He was a master mariner in the Merchant Navy and an experienced sailor with his own specially built yacht, the *Suhaili*. His heroes were men like Sir Francis Drake and Horatio Nelson, and he was a great patriot. When he made his round-the-world voyage in 1968, he had two main aims: to break Sir Francis Chichester's record by sailing nonstop around the globe and, crucially, to beat the French yachtsmen who were taking part in the race.

For both Naomi James and Robin Knox-Johnston, the challenge had two dimensions: They had to sail a boat 30,000 miles single-handed, through some of the roughest seas in the world, and they had to cope with months of solitude. Knox-Johnston knew a lot about big ships, but he did not really think of himself as a classic yachtsman. He had far more experience than James, however; she had never traveled farther than the Canary Islands. Her goal was slightly less intimidating because she always planned to make several stops en route, but for someone so new to sailing and with no solo experience whatsoever, the challenge was awesome.

Fortunately, she proved to be a very good sailor and a quick learner. She worked out how to manage the ship on her own and how to repair it when things went wrong. When, at one point, James discovered that her navigational calculations had gone awry because she was mixing up latitude and longitude, she didn't panic. After she realized her mistake, she never made it again.

Her moment of crisis came as she was approaching Cape Horn, the southernmost tip of South America, a notoriously dangerous stretch of water. It was 169 days into her voyage, and things were not looking good. The Southern Ocean was growing increasingly stormy, and James wasn't sure that her boat could take it. After one particularly close shave, she was terrified that her main mast might snap. Things were so serious that she started to think about temporarily abandoning her attempt and returning to New Zealand for a refit. Then, suddenly, at 5:00 in the morning on the February 27, the *Express Crusader* capsized.

James was in her bunk half asleep when debris started flying all over the cabin. The boat righted itself, and James struggled onto deck, expecting the worst. The spinnaker was gone, sails were dragging in the water, and the radio aerial had been wrenched from its socket—but, amazingly, the mainmast was intact. It was pandemonium. All around, enormous waves towered above her boat and threatened to smash it to pieces. In between desperate hours at the bilge pumps, she attempted to steer through chaotic seas. The *Express Crusader* was carried along, surfing the waves; any moment now, James thought, could be her last.

Gradually, however, the weather eased, allowing James to steal some sleep and make a few desperate repairs. Then she had her epiphany: If her boat could survive capsizing in the Southern Ocean, it would be able to take her all the way home. James realized that it was her own fear that was making Cape Horn seem so impossible. For the moment at least, she had conquered that fear. Survive this, she thought, and you can survive anything.

For Robin Knox-Johnston, Cape Horn was also the crux of his voyage. By the time he got within sight, his boat, too, was in poor shape. The self-steering mechanism had broken, forcing him to spend long watches at the wheel. He had had a lot of bad weather and worried that more was coming. Knox-Johnston was still mentally strong, but he was exhausted, and there was only one question at the front of his mind: Why was he putting himself through this?

In moments of crisis, both sailors called on outside forces for help. For Robin Knox-Johnston, this meant God; sailors, he said, were superstitious or God-fearing, or both. Naomi James wasn't sure about God; her faith, she wrote, was based on her background, her family, her friends, and above all her husband. Wherever she was, she felt that he was with her, giving her the strength to carry on, even when it seemed impossible.

She spoke to her husband on the radio as often as possible and sought his advice whenever she was in difficulty. Of course, Rob could not man the radio for 24 hours a day, so when she could not speak to him directly, she tried to imagine what he and her other "invisible mentor," Chay Blyth, would have done in the same circumstances. This idea of an invisible mentor is something common to several women explorers. In the back of their minds, they have a real person who has given them real help in the past and who can be called on mentally when they need help again.

Robin Knox-Johnston had his heroes, but he did not have any invisible mentors—or, for that matter, anyone to call on at home. He was sustained, however, by an intense feeling of competition. Knox-Johnston was convinced that Britain's maritime history made it right and fitting that a British sailor should set the record for sailing solo around the world. His main rival was the great yachtsman Bernard

Moitessier, and he used his fear that a Frenchman might beat him to push himself on. James, by contrast, didn't seem to realize that that she had a Polish rival and never mentioned Chojnowska-Liskiewicz in her account.

For both of them, dealing with the solitude was almost as much a trial as the sailing itself. James had a slightly easier time of it, breaking her voyage in South Africa and the Falkland Islands. She also had a good radio that functioned most of the time, unlike Robin's. In a peculiar way, James used her enforced solitude at sea to examine her character on dry land. She was a very quiet, reserved person who often felt uncomfortable around strangers. She did not like small talk and worried about the social obligations that she would be put under when she returned to Britain. Her months at sea proved to her that it was possible to survive without other people and though she longed for Rob, she wondered if there wasn't an important lesson here. James did not want to spend her future as a recluse, but this voyage demonstrated that it was possible to opt out of normal society and live much more quietly.

Knox-Johnston was equally anxious about the solitude. Before he set sail he was examined by a psychologist and, though he was given a clean bill of health, he occasionally wondered about his sanity. His radio wasn't as reliable as James's, and he found that conversations with other people only made him feel more depressed afterward. He was more gregarious than James; prior to this expedition, he had spent most of the previous decade in the company of ships' crews.

Some of his coping strategies—listening to music, reading voraciously, keeping a personal diary—were the same as James's, but in other respects he was very different. Knox-Johnston listened avidly to world news but James was totally uninterested. When she got bored, she carved chess pieces and read books on antiques; Knox-Johnston preferred the classics of world literature and Bertrand Russell's *History of Western Philosophy.* He also personalized his boat to a much greater degree: *Suhaili* was very definitely female, but the sail, *The Big Fellow,* was definitely male and so was *The Admiral,* his nickname for the self-steering mechanism. James was much less sentimental about her yacht; it was simply a means to an end. She reserved her emotional energy for people rather than machines.

Long-distance solo sailing is in some ways like mountaineering: It is such a singular activity that it is risky to make generalizations. In certain respects, however, Knox-Johnston and James did conform to typical gender patterns. His insistent self-reliance and his competitiveness are common male traits; her mental toughness and strong survival instinct are common to female sailors. What they both shared was an incredible drive to succeed, a quality present in all the great explorers.

What They Did Next

Naomi James

James returned to Britain to great acclaim. She wrote two books about her solo voyage and continued to sail, often with her husband, Rob. Tragically, he died in a yachting disaster in 1983, just a few weeks before she gave birth to their daughter. After that her life changed significantly; she went back to university and studied philosophy. Today she lives in Ireland and has given up sailing.

Robin Knox-Johnston

After his record-breaking voyage around the world, Knox-Johnson continued to be deeply involved with sailing. He was Britain's Yachtsman of the Year three times and continued to race into his 60s. Today he runs a successful business building marinas and holds various posts within the nautical world.

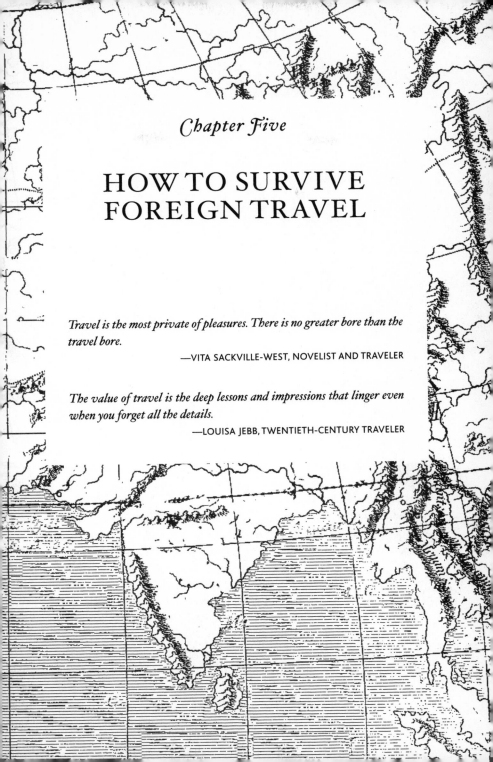

Chapter Five

HOW TO SURVIVE
FOREIGN TRAVEL

Travel is the most private of pleasures. There is no greater bore than the travel bore.

—VITA SACKVILLE-WEST, NOVELIST AND TRAVELER

The value of travel is the deep lessons and impressions that linger even when you forget all the details.

—LOUISA JEBB, TWENTIETH-CENTURY TRAVELER

In *My Antarctic Honeymoon,* Jenny Darlington recounts the story of a team of scientists who set up a meteorological station 20 miles away from the main hut. Two men are left in charge; the weather deteriorates and radio contact is lost. The others try to send out a relief expedition, but bad weather holds them back. Then suddenly one of the weathermen bursts through the door, in terrible shape. He tells everyone that his partner has fallen into a crevasse and that the last thing he asked for was a knife.

Immediately all the men rush out to rescue him, ignoring the danger and the very low odds that their colleague is still alive. Darlington worries for her husband, Harry, one of the would-be rescuers, but she also reflects on the incident in a brutally honest way. This is a moment, she says, when the genders behave very differently. Men are desperate to be heroes, but women are much more rational. A woman would not risk her life, or anyone else's, on a rescue mission that had very little chance of success (though in this case, they were successful).

This idea that women have a stronger survival instinct occurs elsewhere in exploration literature. Take Nina Mazuchelli. In the 1870s, she accompanied her husband, a British army chaplain, on one of the earliest European expeditions to the Himalayas. After several weeks trekking through the foothills, their large party of porters and guides was growing desperate and mutinous. They had little food, little fire-wood, and little hope.

Suddenly Mazuchelli leapt up. "With a woman's natural instinct I believe I arrived at the only safe course to pursue. 'Let us return at once' I cried, stamping the snow with my foot in my vehemence. 'It is the only thing to save us.'"

They turned back and a few days later found a village where they were able to buy food. Mazuchelli and her party survived and returned to tell the tale.

Why would women have a stronger survival reflex? Nicolette Milnes-Walker, the sailor and psychotherapist, argues that they are less likely to crack up than men in extreme situations. She claims that women are less selfish because, whether married or not, they are pro-grammed to be caregivers. This means that they will not allow them-selves to die because they have so many other people to live for. Men, however, are less likely to think about their dependents, even when they appear to be acting altruistically.

This is an intriguing idea; throughout the history of exploration, women have faced prejudice and sometimes been called the weaker sex, but are they in fact better at surviving crises?

This chapter looks at how to survive and thrive in the exploration game. It begins with two maritime survival stories, a century and a half apart, in which women were forced to call on all their inner strength to endure against the odds.

SHIPWRECKED OFF THE BARBARY COAST

In 1818, at the age of 35, Eliza Bradley boarded a boat for Tenerife with her husband, Captain James Bradley. This was the first time that she had accompanied him on a voyage, and she was the only woman among 32 crew and passengers. During the early years of their marriage, Eliza had tried to persuade James to change to a safer profession, but he had refused.

The care of life is the strongest passion in the human breast; it continues with us to the last moment of existence; the miseries one feels may weaken it perhaps, but rarely extinguish it.

—ELIZA BRADLEY

The first few weeks of the voyage were uneventful, but then, off the coast of North Africa, they were caught in a terrible five-day storm that wrecked their ship. Fortunately, they had a lifeboat; less fortunately, they landed on the notorious Barbary Coast, where if the heat didn't kill you the local tribesmen frequently did.

They had no weapons and few supplies. Their only hope was that local people would find them—but that meant almost certainly being held for ransom. Finally, a group of Arab tribesmen appeared and, as per the script, attacked and captured them. They separated Eliza from her husband and put her on the back of a camel; the men were forced to march across the desert on a diet of roast locusts and water from a rancid goatskin.

James Bradley fell into despair, but his wife found comfort in the Bible that she had saved from the shipwreck. "I shall not die but live; and declare the works of the Lord" said the book of Psalms, and Eliza Bradley made heartfelt attempts to believe it.

Whether through chivalry or simply because she was a greater prize, Eliza received better treatment. They allowed her to sleep in a tent and gave her marginally better food. Eventually, after several weeks, they arrived at a small settlement, where Eliza was spat upon and stoned. It would become her home for the next four months.

"Who de do Christiano?" an old man greeted her. Evidently, he had learned a little English from previous captives. He told Eliza that she would not be allowed to leave until the British consul paid a significant ransom. In the meantime, she was allowed to wander around the village and observe the tribe. For two or three hours every day, she collected snails and groundnuts for food. Some of the Arab women treated her with compassion; others continued to abuse her; she, in turn, noticed that wives were often treated very badly by their husbands.

Throughout the whole experience, Eliza's main comfort was her Bible. She was permitted to keep it but, she was never allowed to read in the presence of her captors and their families. Just in case the Arabs changed their minds, she buried it in the sand whenever she left her tent.

Finally, after several months, a letter arrived from her husband informing her that he and the others were safe and that a reward of $700 had been offered for her return. Eliza was taken on a 700-mile march to the coast, but her ordeal wasn't quite over; as she moved from town to town local people came to stare at her and insult her.

When they arrived at Mogadore, in modern day Morocco, the British consul handed over the money and Eliza was reunited with her husband. All the crew had survived, but some were in very poor physical shape. After several weeks of daily baths and gallons of goat's milk, Eliza felt her strength returning and was able to board a ship back to England. Forty days later she was hugging her friends on the quayside in Liverpool. Although sometimes she, too, had despaired, Eliza Bradley was able to survive her experience through a mixture of sheer resilience and religious faith. God, she was sure, had saved her and to God she owed her thanks.

The second survival story took place over a century later in the Pacific Ocean. This time the husband and wife were not separated, and the local delicacy was . . . aquatic.

ABANDONING SHIP IN THE PACIFIC

In the spring of 1973, a British couple, Maurice and Maralyn Bailey, set out from Panama for the Galápagos Islands in their yacht, *Auralyn*. It was supposed to be a short pleasure trip for a couple, who a few years earlier had sold their house, given up their jobs, and taken to the sea. They had made some tentative plans to meet some friends at the Galápagos, but nothing was too organized. Life in those days for the Baileys was free and easy.

Early one morning, several days into their voyage, they noticed a large fishing ship on the horizon. Then a few hours later, something unexpected happened. A wounded whale surfaced nearby and smashed a hole in the underside of their yacht. They tried vainly to plug the leak with a blanket, but the damage was too great, and they had to abandon ship.

The Baileys didn't panic; rather, they worked calmly to inflate their life raft and small rubber dinghy. After all, they were sailing in very busy shipping lanes; it wouldn't be too long before they were rescued. They filled their life raft and a small inflatable dinghy with 20 days' worth of food and water and then watched as their boat sank.

Over the next week, they developed a routine for meals: a couple of biscuits for breakfast, a handful of peanuts for lunch, and a can of hot food at night. Their liquid allowance was a shared bottle of water mixed with Coffeemate. They had managed to salvage only two books and two dictionaries, so they spent a lot of time trying to remember the plots of their favorite novels. Taking a cue from a story they had heard about a prisoner of war enduring solitary confinement in Korea, they began to design a new yacht to replace *Auralyn*. Hope had kept the POW sane, and they sustained themselves by thinking about the future.

Although the Baileys were convinced that they would be rescued, it was a grim existence. The life raft was so small that only one person could lie down, so they slept in three-hour shifts. Maurice became more and more depressed, but though Maralyn cried a lot, she never lost the unshakable faith that somehow they would survive.

Then suddenly, on the eighth day, they saw a ship. Quickly they swung into action: Maurice lit their precious flares and Maralyn frantically waved her yellow oilskin jacket. But the ship sailed on. Over the next four and a half months they sighted six more ships, but none came to their rescue.

When their canned food ran out, they were forced to improvise. They cut safety pins in half to make hooks and started fishing. There was plenty to catch, but as the weeks went on, Maurice grew thinner and thinner. So they turned to a much larger and friendlier source of nourishment: sea turtles.

At first, the turtles had been their friends, swimming gently around their boat, but desperate times required desperate measures, and eventually their pets became their prey. Maralyn developed into a skilled butcher, and there wasn't much of the turtle that they didn't eat. Choice cuts included the heart, liver, kidneys, shoulders, and pelvic region. Best of all was the gooey greenish fat from the inside of the shell. One day, they caught a female; to their delight, they found dozens of eggs in her belly.

Privately, Maurice began to doubt that they would ever be rescued, after so many ships had passed them by. He developed a hacking cough and salt sores on his back; Maralyn didn't tell him quite how bad they were. Then one day disaster struck again when they punctured one of dinghy's air chambers with a fishhook; they managed to mend it by sacrificing one of their water drums, but the repair didn't last long, and they had to spend half an hour every night pumping seawater out of their dinghy. To add to the torment, sharks circled their life raft and head-butted them from underneath, leaving Maurice and Maralyn covered in bruises.

Suddenly, on day 117, Maralyn spotted a boat on the horizon; it was the first they had seen for almost two months. Amazingly, as she waved her jacket, it turned toward them. Before they knew what was happening, they found themselves being winched up into a Korean fishing ship. At first, the captain was very suspicious and accused them of being Russian spies, but they managed to convince him that they were just an ordinary British couple who had been shipwrecked.

When the captain radioed his company in Seoul, news of their dramatic rescue was transmitted all over the world; the Baileys received dozens of messages of support. Finally the boat reached Honolulu, where Maurice and Maralyn disembarked, already plotting their return to the sea in *Auralyn II*.

Reviewing the medical aspects of their story some months later, Captain John Waters from the Institute of Naval Studies noted that though they were both very weak, Maralyn was in much better physical condition at the end. Women use less energy than men and generally have greater fat stores that can be drawn upon in starvation situations. Maralyn's periods had stopped for three months but they started again before her rescue, as if her body had adjusted to the new conditions.

Maralyn in particular had made a real effort to keep their morale high, telling her husband stories, making up games, and creating reasons for mini-celebrations, even though they had little to be happy about. Maurice later acknowledged that she coped with their ordeal better than he, both physically and mentally.

Even though women like Maralyn Bailey and Eliza Bradley show tremendous resilience, there is no doubt that travel and exploration are dangerous activities; few explorers manage to get away completely unscathed. In fact, you can say that injury and disease are occupational hazards for the explorer, which only the exceptionally lucky manage to avoid.

THE RISKS OF EXPLORATION

The Victorian traveler Mary Kingsley was shot in the ankle with a muzzle-loading gun filled with scrap metal. It took months to clean the wound and remove old bits of cooking pot.

HOW TO CATCH A SHARK WITHOUT A HOOK

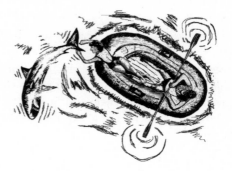

Allow the shark to circle your boat.
Grab it by the tail and haul it on board.
Wrap it up in a towel.
Bludgeon it to death with a heavy object.

Note: Maralyn Bailey's method worked well with two-foot sharks, but it is not recommended for larger varieties.

Over the course of almost 50 years of flying, the pioneering American pilot Jackie Cochran crashed several times and was almost asphyxiated when, on one flight, carbon monoxide leaked into the cockpit. Her most dangerous moment at the controls occurred, however, when she suffered an extreme abdominal blockage caused by several years of a very poor diet. Fortunately, she had a copilot on board.

The famous desert explorer of the nineteen thirties, Freya Stark, repeatedly fell ill on her travels. At various times she suffered from malaria, dengue fever, sandfly fever, dysentery, and boils. Her most dangerous injury, however, came at the age of 12, long before she started traveling, when in a freak accident her hair was trapped in a mill at her mother's silk factory. She suffered massive injuries to her scalp and the right side of her face that left her permanently disfigured.

Many other women have suffered on their travels, but perhaps the queen of the survivors is the modern Irish travel writer Dervla Murphy. During an account of her expedition to Russia in 2002, *Through Siberia by Accident,* she included a list of over 17 serious illnesses and injuries that she had endured over many years on the trail. Low points included:

Broken ribs and a scorpion bite in Afghanistan
Brucellosis in India
A dislocated knee in Ethiopia
Gout in Madagascar
Concussion in Romania
Malaria in Zimbabwe
Tick-bite fever in South Africa
Multiple injuries in Siberia

Dervla is living proof of the old phrase, That which doesn't kill you makes you stronger.

One way to mitigate the dangers of travel is to equip yourself with as big a first aid kit as you can find, or so thought the American explorer May French Sheldon. By the end of the nineteenth century, companies like Burroughs Wellcome and Co. were offering explorers a wide range of compressed medicines in tablet form. When Sheldon led an expedition through East Africa in 1891, she wore a medicine belt around her waist with no less than 45 such preparations, several of which look distinctly toxic:

Sulphonal tabloids	For insomnia
Lead and opium tabloids	For dysentery and diarrhea
Arsenicus acid tabloids	For malaria
Forced March tabloids	Taken every 2 hours to act as a stimulant and to ward off craving for food ("Very effectual," Sheldon commented.)
Livingstone's rousers	Tonic antimalarial pills invented by David Livingstone
Saccharin tabloids	In lieu of sugar for sweetening food and drink
Nitrate of Silver	For cauterizing wounds

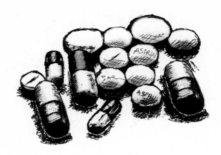

Considering the size of her pharmacopeia and her predilection for Forced March tablets, it is not surprising that for the majority of the expedition Sheldon slept for just two hours a night.

It is easy enough to take pills from a medicine kit, but what happens when things get so serious that you need an operation? In 1961, a doctor at a Russian research station in Antarctica, Leonid Rogozov, famously operated on himself after developing appendicitis. One of the most extraordinary survival stories of recent years revolves around Jerri Nielsen, a female doctor at an Antarctic research station, who discovered that she, too, needed urgent medical help.

COLD COMFORT

By 1998, hospital doctor Jerri Nielsen had hit rock bottom. A troubled marriage followed by an acrimonious divorce had left her estranged from her children and at war with her former husband. When she saw an advertisement for a physician's job in Antarctica, she knew that it was for her. She would swap the emergency room at a large mid-American hospital for a scientific base at the South Pole. It would be an escape, a year away from the friction and stress of her domestic life, the perfect "geographical cure" for an unhappy doctor.

Nielsen arrived at the South Pole in November 1998, and, at first, all went well. Like many others before her, she fell in love with the unique landscape of Antarctica and found it deeply spiritual. In February, preparations began for the long, dark polar winter. The base's scientific and technical staff was reduced to a core of 41 over-winterers, of whom Nielsen was one.

She looked forward to a few months of treating cold-related injuries, the winter blues, and whatever minor accidents might occur. Then in early March 1999, barely a month after the last plane had flown out of Antarctica, she found a small lump in her right breast.

She didn't panic immediately. Nielsen had had lumps before, and they had always gone away. This one, however, proved to be different. A month later, it was still there, and it was growing.

Nielsen knew that it would be virtually impossible to remove such a large tumor, because of the risks of developing a postoperative infection. If it became as big as she thought it might, she couldn't possibly operate on herself, and there was no one else on the base with any real medical training. She did have one crucial advantage, though, over her Russian predecessor Dr. Rogozov: the Internet. Nielsen immediately began corresponding with a radiologist in the United States. Initially the radiologist advised Nielsen that her symptoms sounded

more like a number of fibrocysts clumped together than a tumor, but the lump kept on growing, and Nielsen began to worry about what would happen if she became too sick to perform her duties as the base doctor.

In early June, she told her bosses in the United States about her condition. They put her in touch with some cancer specialists, who advised her to draw some fluid from the lump in order to determine whether it was a cyst or a tumor. By this time, Nielsen felt that she had no choice but to tell everyone on the base. She put on a brave face and made a public announcement; only to her closest friends did she reveal the true extent of her fear. With the assistance of one of the base electricians, she attempted to drain fluid from the lump, but when the needle went in, it hit a solid mass.

So it was a tumor, but was it benign or malignant? The cancer specialists in the United States asked her to perform a biopsy, using whatever equipment she could find. Everyone on the base played a role, some assisting her with the operation, others cobbling together a communications system to transmit video images back the United States.

Nielsen herself performed the procedure, assisted by Walt the welder. The images were transmitted back to the United States, but they just weren't clear enough for anyone to make a proper diagnosis. Everyone knew that it was impossible to evacuate Nielsen, but there was a slim chance of organizing an air drop to bring in more drugs and medical equipment. Nothing went smoothly, though. Twenty-two hours before the plane was due to fly over the base, a fire in the power plant killed the lights for eight nerve-wracking minutes.

The blaze was extinguished and an emergency generator came online, but the station chief made another, equally uncomfortable announcement: A computer hacker was trying to get onto their network, jeopardizing their connection to the Internet, Nielsen's emotional and medical lifeline. Fortunately for Nielsen, the hacker didn't succeed.

When the plane finally arrived it was −92° F. Six packages were dropped; five survived, but the most expensive item, an ultrasound scanner to help measure the tumor, was smashed to pieces. Nielsen began a course of combined hormonal treatment to slow down the growth of the lump, but it had the nasty side effect of initiating menopause.

Back home in America, the press got hold of the story and began feverish speculation about the identity of the patient. At first they didn't know that it was the base doctor, but eventually reporters found her parents and Nielsen's name was revealed.

At the end of July, Nielsen's worst fears were realized. After a second biopsy, the specialists confirmed that it was a malignant tumor. Using drugs that had survived the air-drop, Nielsen began a course of chemotherapy, under the care of a new cancer specialist, Kathy Miller, thousands of miles away at the other end of a video link.

At first the treatment seemed to work. The tumor shrank, and Nielsen was able to cope with the drugs, but then, after a couple of weeks, the tumor started to grow again. In spite of all the pressures, Nielsen was remarkably resilient. When her hair began to fall out, she shaved it all off, surrounded by her friends at an impromptu party. But the chemotherapy drugs were relentlessly taking their toll. The walls of her veins began to collapse; when she tried changing drugs, she reacted badly and grew even weaker.

By early October, daylight was creeping over the horizon. It could not have come sooner. With Nielsen's condition deteriorating by the day, an emergency flight was arranged at the earliest possible moment. On October 16, a plane touched down and within minutes she was on her way to New Zealand and then on to America, where she shortly began a series of operations. Surgeons removed the tumor, but Jerri developed a postoperative infection that almost killed her.

Eventually Nielsen was nursed back to health. She wrote a successful book, had her story adapted for TV, and made dozens of speeches about surviving cancer. Unlike Richard Byrd or August Courthauld, two earlier polar explorers who had been stuck in their bases, Nielsen didn't have to face her situation on her own. She was given invaluable support by her friends and colleagues at the base and was in constant email contact with her parents and brothers. However, it was terrible ordeal, made even worse by the fact that, as a doctor, she couldn't hide from the truth. Only someone of enormous character could have survived such pressure. The simple lesson that it taught her, as she wrote afterward, was that when things go wrong, everyone has the capacity to draw on enormous reserves of strength. When in 2005 her cancer returned; she fought on courageously, but in 2009 she died at the age of 57.

RIP

Jerri Nielsen's was an extraordinary case, but there is no doubt that exploration can be very dangerous. It is no surprise that greatest number of deaths has occurred at altitude, in planes or on mountainsides.

The Perils of Pioneering

> *There are old pilots and there are bold pilots but there are no old bold pilots.*
>
> —ANONYMOUS PILOT'S PROVERB

Any woman who took up flying in the early years had no choice but to be bold: The only question was, for how long would she survive?

1912
Harriet Quimby was America's first licensed pilot and the first woman to fly the English Channel. Fewer than three months later on July 1,

1912, she died at an aviation meet in Boston. According to a contemporary report in the *New York Times,* she and a passenger were flying in a Blériot monoplane when suddenly "the machine turned almost perpendicular in the air, and the two bodies turned over and over in the air as they shot downwards." Neither survived, but their pilotless plane glided down and made a perfect landing on some mudflats before spinning over onto its back.

1922

Elsa Andersson was the first female pilot and parachutist in Sweden. She died in 1922 during an air display when, on her third jump, her parachute failed to open until she was very close to the treetops. She hit the ground with an audible bump and died immediately.

1937

Amelia Earhart remains one of the most famous pilots in the history of aviation. The resilience of her legend is partly to do with the mysterious circumstances of her disappearance while on a second attempt to fly around the world. Her body and that of her copilot were never found, prompting a spate of bizarre rumors: Some said that she had survived and worked as a spy against Japan, others that she had survived and was in fact working *for* the Japanese, and others that the Japanese had found and executed her. The strangest theory of all, sensationally published in a book in 1970, was that she had returned to the United States anonymously and taken on a new identity as a New Jersey banker. In fact, the banker in question had nothing to do with Earhart; she sued the book's author and won substantial damages.

1941

Amy Johnson, Britain's answer to Amelia Earhart, was another aviation casualty who died in slightly mysterious circumstances. At the beginning of World War II, she joined Britain's Air Transport Auxiliary, flying planes around Britain for the Royal Air Force. In January 1941, she was on her way from Blackpool to Oxford, when severe weather forced her to abandon her plane and bail out into the Thames Estuary.

She survived the parachute jump and was sighted in the freezing waters, but a rescue attempt failed and her body was never recovered.

The Perils of High Altitude

There is no doubt that mountaineering, and particularly high-altitude mountaineering, is one of the most dangerous forms of exploration. The combined effects of severe weather and extreme environmental conditions make the risk of accident very high.

K2 is one of the most famous challenges in mountaineering. It is a few yards shorter than Everest but is unquestionably harder to climb. There is no yak route up K2: Anyone who takes it on has to be at the top of his or her game. The statistics are frightening: Between 1954, when it was first climbed by an Italian team, and 2003, 200 people reached the summit and 53 died on the attempt, over one in four. The mortality rate for women climbers is no higher than for men, but there was a period in the 1980s and 1990s when it seemed that most of the world's top female climbers had died either on K2 or a few years later. K2 was always a mountain that had attracted melodramatic soubriquets, the "Savage

Mountain" and the "Killer Mountain" being the best known. Continuing the theme, journalists started to write about the "curse of K2," a fatal spell on any woman who tried to climb it.

THE CURSE OF K2

JUNE 1986
The Polish climber Wanda Rutkiewicz becomes the first woman to reach the summit of K2 and lives to tell the tale. On the same day, the French climber Liliane Barrard also summits K2 with her husband, Maurice. They both die on the descent.

AUGUST 1986
The British climber Julie Tullis reaches the summit after several attempts. On the way down, she and her partner are trapped in a storm. Tullis dies.

MAY 12–13, 1992
Wanda Rutkiewicz dies climbing Kanchenjunga, six years after her ascent of K2.

AUGUST 1992
French climber Chantal Maudit climbs K2.

AUGUST 1995
Alison Hargreaves becomes the first British woman to reach the summit of K2 without using supplementary oxygen. She dies on the descent.

MAY 1998
Chantal Maudit dies on Dhaulagiri in Nepal, six years after she climbed K2.

In recent years, the curse seems to have been lifted with leading climbers Nives Meroi and Edurne Pasaban reaching the summit and living to tell the tale for several years afterward. The simple fact is that all mountains are dangerous. When the particular perils of high altitude are added, the risks increase.

THE "BLESSINGS OF EXPLORATION"

Alexandra David-Néel lived to almost 101 and was still studying Buddhist texts in her 80s. She renewed her passport shortly before her death.

Ella Maillart lived to 94 and was still taking tour parties to remote parts of Asia in her 80s.

Freya Stark lived to 100 and was still traveling in her 90s.

Mrs. Victoria Bruce, the driver and pilot, lived to 94 and was still test-driving cars at the age of 79.

Annie Smith Peck, the mountaineer, lived to the age of 84 and was still traveling the world in her 80s.

Although it is easy to dwell on the dangers of exploration, it is also important to remember that a lot of women explorers did survive their travels, and some even went on to live for a remarkably long time.

What happens though if you do not want to keep on going into your 80s? Or, in other words, is there life after exploration?

NEXT . . .

Figuring out what to do next can be surprisingly difficult for anyone who has dedicated their life to exploration. After years of hardship in

the field, interspersed with brief bursts of adulation from the public and the media, it is often difficult to come home from the hill. Although you might be able to persuade people to finance your expeditions, it is not so easy to get anyone to sponsor your retirement.

Some famous male explorers, such as Fridtjof Nansen and Hiram Bingham, went into politics, but few women followed. Pilot Jackie Cochran tried and failed to become a Republican Congresswoman. May French Sheldon and Mary Kingsley were more successful at becoming important voices on the African question, but when Sheldon tried to carve herself a huge plantation in Africa, she failed miserably. Gertrude Bell was probably the female explorer who had the greatest political impact, playing a major role in drawing up the frontiers of the modern Middle East.

Some women travelers were very successful at building second careers: The British yachtswoman Clare Francis gave up the sea to become a bestselling novelist, and the American climber Arlene Blum gave up high-altitude mountaineering to resume an important scientific career. Sarah Hobson, the British girl who traveled through Iran dressed as a boy, became a filmmaker, and Marie Herbert became a wilderness quest leader.

Writing is a very obvious way to both finance your travels while you're still involved and to profit from them after you have finished. There have been many great books by female explorers—though few of them, it has to be said, have sold as well as classic men's accounts.

Just as traditionally there has been a lot of prejudice against women travelers, so, too, has there been a lack of interest in women's travel books, no matter how good they are.

Good books can bring you back from the brink or gain you posthumous fame: The pioneering aviator Beryl Markham was living in Africa in semi-poverty when the republication of *West with the Night* in the 1980s brought her a new audience and much-needed new royalties. Margaret Fountaine was a long-forgotten Victorian butterfly collector until 1978 when, according to the terms of her will, her diaries were opened for the first time. A few years later, they were sensationally published revealing her extraordinary life and bringing her posthumous fame.

The most successful female travel writer was probably Freya Stark. In her lifetime, she published 24 travel books and autobiographies and released 8 volumes of letters. She succeeded because she was both a great explorer, whose adventures were worth reading about, and a witty writer with a light touch.

More generally, it is this lightness of touch, combined with humor and a fascination the stories of new people, that distinguishes female

---

SOME TRAVEL BOOKS WRITTEN BY WOMEN

With Pole and Paddle Down the Zambezi by Jessica Currie, 1918

On Sledge and Horseback to Outcast Siberian Lepers by Kate Marsden, 1893

To Lake Tanganyika in a Bath Chair by Annie B. Hore, 1886

Tight Corners of My Adventurous Life by Ethel Brilliana Tweedy, 1933

A Scamper around the World by Lady F. N. Moss, 1902

"Indiscretions" of Lady Susan by Lady Susan Townley, 1922

Station Amusements in New Zealand by Lady Mary Anne Barker, 1873

Roughing It in the Bush by Susanna Moodie, 1852

---

from male exploration literature. Women's books can be just as dramatic as men's, but they rarely lapse into kind of gung-ho "painography" that has been a characteristic of male explorers from Robert Peary to Joe Simpson—and which, it has to be added, the public seem to love.

Women explorers can suffer from the same sense-of-humor failure as male explorers when it comes to their book titles. As you can see from the list on the previous page, a few of the great titles from women's travel literature have obviously never passed through the irony detector.

THE FUTURE . . .

What lies ahead beyond the far horizon for women explorers? What will the travelogues of the future be? Apart from going deep into the bowels of the Earth or to the depths of the oceans, there are no great geographical prizes left (that we know of, at least). This, of course, is not to say that the whole of the Earth has been thoroughly mapped, climbed, photographed, and explored. Far from it. There are thousands of unclimbed mountains and untrodden passes and regions that have barely been visited. There is much to do on Earth, but whether future travelers will be able to capture the public imagination in the same way as Freya Stark or Gertrude Bell remains to be seen.

If there is going to be a new golden age, it will probably be in space exploration. Valentina Tereshkova was the first woman in space, launched into orbit in 1963 on Vostok 6. Sally Ride became the first American woman in space in 1983, when she orbited Earth in the space shuttle *Challenger*. Today dozens more women have been into space; sadly, three have given their lives for the experience. The pace of exploration has quickened with India and China as new but vigorous entrants into the space race. The costs are huge, and the technology isn't quite there yet, but the "Golden Age of Space Exploration" is yet to come. When Lillias Campbell's classic Victorian handbook *Hints to Lady Travellers at Home and Abroad* is updated, undoubtedly there will have to be a section on space etiquette and how to maintain your dignity in zero gravity.

EPILOGUE

Does exploration really tell you anything about the differences between women and men?

> Women are better survivors — but try telling that to Joe Simpson or Ernest Shackleton.

> Women are more interested in people than places — but try telling that to Eric Newby or Patrick Leigh Fermor.

> Women are less competitive than men — but try telling that to Wanda Rutkiewicz or Ellen MacArthur.

> Women don't like taking risks — but try telling that to Amelia Earhart or Rosita Forbes.

In the end, there are very few generalizations that cannot be contradicted, except to say that women explorers are far less well known than men.

Ultimately, perhaps the truth is that there are many more similarities between adventurous men and adventurous women than there are differences. They all have to be risk takers, they all have to be survivors, they all have to be interested in people as well as in places, and, above all, they all have to be just a little bit different from the rest of us mere mortals.

As the old Persian saying goes:

Travel is a form of madness.

BIBLIOGRAPHY

PRIMARY SOURCES

Angeville, Henriette d'. *My Ascent of Mont Blanc*. Paris, 1987.

Arnesen, Liv, and Ann Bancroft. *No Horizon Is So Far*. New York, 2003.

Bailey, Maralyn and Maurice. *117 Days Adrift*. London, 1988.

Bancroft, Ann (and Nancy Loewen). *Four to the Pole*. North Haven, Connecticut, 2001.

Bell, Gertrude. *The Desert and the Sown*. London, 1907.

——. *Amurath to Amurath*. London, 1911.

——. *The Letters of Gertrude Bell*. London, 1927.

Bird, Isabella. *A Lady's Life in the Rocky Mountains*. London, 1879.

——. *Journeys in Persia and Kurdistan*. London 1891.

Blum, Arlene. *Annapurna: A Woman's Place Is on Top*. San Francisco, 1980.

——. *Breaking Trail*. New York, 2005.

Blunt, Lady Anne. *Bedoin Tribes of the Euphrates*. London, 1879.

Bradley, Eliza. *An Authentic Account of the Sufferings of Mrs. Eliza Bradley*. London, 1824.

Bruce, Mrs. Victor. *Nine Lives Plus*. London, 1977.

Bulstrode, Beatrix. *A Tour in Mongolia*. London, 1920.

Burton, Lady Isabel. *The Inner Life of Syria*. London, 1875.

Caddick, Helen. *A White Woman in Central Africa*. London, 1900.

Campbell-Davies, Lillias. *Hints to Lady Travellers*. London, 1889.

Caton-Thompson, Gertrude. *Mixed Memoirs*. Gateshead, 1983.

Cochran, Jackie (and Maryann Bucknum Brinley). *An Autobiography*. New York, 1987.

Cole, Mrs. H. W. *A Lady's Tour round Monte Rosa*. London, 1859.

Courtt Treatt, Stella. *Cape to Cairo*. London, 1927.

Craven, Lady Elizabeth. *A Journey through the Crimea to Constantinople*. London, 1789.

Darlington, Jennie. *Antarctic Honeymoon*. London, 1957.

David-Néel, Alexandra. *My Journey to Lhasa*. London, 1927.

———. *Tibetan Journey.* Paris, 1933.

Davidson, Lillias Campbell. *Hints to Lady Travellers at Home and Abroad.* London, 1889.

Davison, Ann. *My Ship Is So Small.* London, 1956.

Deacock, Antonia. *No Purdah in Padam.* London, 1960.

Dixie, Florence. *Across Patagonia.* London, 1880.

Dodwell, Christina. *Travels with Fortune.* London, 1979.

———. *Travels with Pegasus.* London, 1989.

———. *An Explorer's Handbook.* London, 1984.

Earhart, Amelia. *The Fun of It.* New York, 1932.

Eberhardt, Isabelle. *In the Shadow of Islam.* Paris, 1993.

Fleming, Peter. *News from Tartary.* London, 1936.

Flowers, Pam. *Alone Across the Arctic.* Portland, Oregon, 2001.

Forbes, Rosita. *The Secret of the Sahara: Kufara.* London, 1921.

———. *Gypsy in the Sun.* London, 1944.

Fountaine, Margaret. *Love Among the Butterflies.* London, 1980.

———. *Butterflies and Later Loves.* London, 1986.

Francis, Clare. *Come Hell or High Water.* London, 1977.

———. *Come Wind or Weather.* London, 1978.

Graham Bower, Ursula. *Naga Path.* London, 1950.

Hall, Mary. *A Woman's Trek from the Cape to Cairo.* London, 1907.

Hamilton, Caroline. *To the Pole.* London, 2000.

Harkness, Ruth. *The Lady and the Panda.* New York, 1938.

Hill, Lynn. *Climbing Free.* New York, 2002.

Herbert, Marie. *The Snow People.* London, 1973.

———. *The Reindeer People.* London, 1976.

Herbert, Kari. *The Explorer's Daughter.* London, 2004.

Herbert, Wally. *A World of Men.* London, 1968.

———. *Eskimos.* Glasgow, 1978.

Hillary, Edmund. *View from the Summit.* London, 1999.

Hobson, Sarah. *Through Persia in Disguise.* London, 1973.

Hore, Annie Boyle. *To Lake Tanganyika in a Bath Chair.* London, 1886.

Hubbard, Mrs. Leonidas. *A Woman's Way through Unknown Labrador.* New York, 1908.

Jackson, Monica. *Tents in the Clouds.* London, 1956.

James, Naomi. *Woman Alone.* London, 1979.

Jebb, Louisa. *By Desert Ways to Baghdad.* London, 1908.

Johnson, Amy. *Skyroads of the World.* London, 1939.

Johnson, Osa. *I Married Adventure.* Philadelphia, 1940.

———. *Bride in the Solomons.* Boston, 1944.

Kingsley, Mary. *Travels in West Africa.* London, 1897.

Knox-Johnston, Robin. *A World of My Own.* London, 1969.

Le Blond, Mrs. Aubrey. *Day In, Day Out*. London, 1928.

Lott, Emmeline. *The English Governess in Egypt*. London, 1866.

Maillart, Ella. *Turkestan Solo*. Paris, 1934.

——. *Forbidden Journey.* Paris, 1937.

——. *The Cruel Way.* London, 1947.

Mansfield, Charlotte. *Via Rhodesia*. London, 1911.

Markham, Beryl. *West with the Night*. Boston, 1942.

Marsden, Kate. *On Sledge and Horseback to Outcast Siberian Lepers*. London, 1893.

Martineau, Harriet. *Eastern Life*. London, 1838.

Mazuchelli, Nina. *The Indian Alps and How We Crossed Them*. London, 1876.

Milnes-Walker, Nicolette. *When I Put Out to Sea*. London, 1973.

Moodie, Susanna. *Roughing it in the Bush*. London, 1852.

Murphy, Dervla. *Cameroon with Egbert*. London, 1989.

——. *In Ethiopia with a Mule*. London, 1968.

——. *Full Tilt*. London, 1965.

——. *On a Shoestring to Coorg*. London, 1976.

——. *Where the Indus Is Young*. London,1977.

——. *Through Siberia by Accident*. London, 2005.

Nielsen, Jerri. *Ice Bound*. New York, 2001.

Peary, Josephine. *My Arctic Journal*. New York 1893.

Peck, Annie. *A Search for the Apex of America*. New York, 1911.

Rjinhart, Susie Carson. *With Tibetans in Tent and Temple*. Edinburgh, 1901.

Sheldon, May French. *Sultan to Sultan*. London, 1892.

Smeeton, Beryl. *Winter Shoes in Springtime*. London, 1961.

——. *The Stars My Blanket*. Victoria, 1995.

Stanhope, Lady Hester. *Memoirs*. London, 1845.

Stark, Freya. *The Valley of the Assassins*. London, 1934.

——. *The Southern Gates of Arabia*. London, 1936.

——. *A Winter in Arabia*. London, 1940.

Swale, Rosie. *Rosie Darling*. London, 1973.

Sykes, Ella. *Through Persia on a Side-Saddle*. London, 1898.

——. *Persia and Its People*. London, 1910.

Taylor, Annie. *The Origin of the Tibet Pioneer Mission*. London, 1894.

Thesiger, Wilfred. *Desert, Marsh and Mountain*. London, 1979.

——. *The Danakil Diary.* London, 1996.

Tullis, Julie. *Clouds from Both Sides*. London, 1986.

West, Vita Sackville. *Passenger to Teheran*. London, 1926.

Wheeler, Sara. *Terra Incognita*. London, 1996.

Workman, Fanny Bullock. *Ice Bound Heights of the Mustagh*. London, 1908.

Wortley Montagu, Lady Mary. *Letters of the Right Honourable Lady Mary Wortley Montagu*. London, 1763.

SECONDARY SOURCES

Boisseau, Tracy. *White Queen*. Bloomington, Indiana, 2004.

Clark, Miles. *High Endeavours*. London, 1991.

Croke, Vicki. *The Lady and the Panda*. New York, 2005.

Foster, Barbara. *Forbidden Journey*. San Francisco, 1989.

Geniesse, Jane Fletcher. *Passionate Nomad*. New York, 1999.

Harper, Stephen. *A Fatal Obsession*. Brighton, 2006.

Hart-Davis, Duff. *Peter Fleming: A Biography*. Oxford, 1987.

Howell, Georgina. *Daughter of the Desert*. London, 2006.

Jordan, Jennifer. *Savage Summit*. New York, 2005.

Lapierre, Alexandra, and Christel Mouchard. *Women Travellers*. Paris, 2007.

Lovell, Mary S. *Straight on Till Morning*. London, 1987.

———. *A Scandalous Life*. London, 1995.

Mackersey, Ian. *Jean Batten*. London, 1999.

Reinisch, Gertrude. *A Caravan of Dreams*. Munich, 1998.

Robinson, Jane. *Wayward Women*. Oxford, 1990.

Russell, Mary. *The Blessings of a Good Thick Skirt*. London, 1994.

INDEX